PERSONAL and PROFESSIONAL TRANSFORMATION

Creating the Life You Want
with Primary Domino Thinking

ANTHONY S. DALLMANN-JONES, PhD

Cover art by Goran

DZ Productions

Fond du Lac, WI

Panama City Beach, FL

www.SuccessHappinessPeace.com

Creating your own health, wealth and happiness
is a power you can master.
This is the greatest secret ever uncovered.

The second greatest secret is to deliberately
develop the willingness to employ that power.
This secret has yet to be discovered.

Table of Contents

THE MISSION

"You can never step into the same river twice."

For a long period of human history the belief was that what was good for the corporation or country was good for the individual. This will never be true again. The Third Reich's and Japan's WWII demise, followed by the eventual fall of the Berlin Wall and Communist Russia, signified the historical and spiritual end of that belief. It was a lie anyway. The truth was that many people made sacrifices for their countries and companies and just wound up getting sacrificed in return. We are too bright to buy into this anymore. The new belief system that has arisen is ever clear: enhancing and empowering the *individual* will make each link in the chain of country/corporation/community/family that much stronger. Healthy and happy people naturally want to help each other, and the gifts they will give are genuine, and not based on the promise of a return.

Ask not what your country can do for you.

Ask not what you can do for your country.

Instead: *Ask what you can do to help yourself!*

The Mission of this book is to empower everyone in the world willing to become a better person through self-transformation. Ambitious? Unreasonable? Crazy? After you read this book and use it and see what happens in your life, you won't think so. You will know what is possible because you will have realized it in your life.

INTRODUCTION

I can best communicate the reason that I have spent years researching, experimenting, writing and rewriting to publish Personal and Professional Transformation by having you do the following exercise:

Imagine a friend of yours sitting across from you with 200 packets of nice crisp $100 bills - a total of $1,000,000 - piled high on a metal table. As you watch, helplessly, your friend pours lighter fluid over the stack and sets it on fire for no apparent reason.

Imagine being there, helpless to do anything - only able to watch all that money burn into ashes.

How would you feel?

Seriously. How would you feel?

What a waste! Right?

Money appears to be just paper, but we know that it is actually human energy stored in a flat green battery. Our pain in seeing the money burn is actually our experiencing intense regret in watching all that potential going up in flames.

As an educator and psychotherapist for over three decades, I have felt that same feeling of regret many times. I feel that way watching great human potential going to waste. I have watched people:

- enduring pain from day to day believing that they have no other choice
- giving up their dreams and experiencing endless, meaningless days believing that there is no other way
- experiencing constant anxiety, boredom or compulsivity believing there is no hope
- escaping to fantasy worlds and/or living in trances where they vicariously live out their lives believing that this is as good as it's going to get

Frankly, it hurts to watch. It especially hurts to watch when you know there is a powerful and effective way to leave behind any and all of those painful states of being. When you know there is a no-fail way for a person to rise from their own ashes no matter how far down they have gone, you have no choice but to find a means to communicate it - especially to those who so desperately need to truly know in their hearts that the Secrets of Self-Transformation process works.

If you read, absorb and utilize what is between the covers of this book, I promise that you will experience success in every area of your life to which you apply it.

This book is for people seeking a potent way to create and command a better life for themselves. To know how to do this is to be *empowered*. To utilize that knowledge *is* power itself.

A lot of books talk about empowerment, but few books show you how to create and utilize power. This one does.

Proof of anything is demonstrated by outcomes, or *results*. I developed the core method known as *Primary Domino Thinking* to provide you with **results**. There is nothing like it.

Many people have utilized *Primary Domino Thinking* to efficiently attain their goals. These goals have included losing weight, creating mood shifts, healing physical problems, lowering golf scores, quitting smoking, creating more wealth, smoothing out relationships, improving sports performance, and many other goals people usually find difficult to accomplish. Again, there is nothing like it.

Your life, as you know it, is about to make a wonderfully exhilarating transition. You will have never known such assurance and power. You will never be powerless again - unless you choose to be - and you won't.

We were born to feel good

I was born to feel good...how about you? But I did not know this was the true reason for being born until about a decade ago. Because I came from a dysfunctional family, I suffered massive *spiritual abuse*, meaning that one sustains heavy damage to one's relationship with the essential and pristine self - it separates one from the *Source*.

I am not feeling sorry for myself or trying to gain your sympathy. I actually have no regrets. I would have preferred not to have gone through all that - I mean, who would consciously choose that path! But I have no regrets, because all of *that* created what I *am* today, and now know why I am here, and how to carry out that *raison d'être*.

One of the reasons I am here is to have a good time teaching you how to *feel good*. Now just what is *feeling good*? YOU have to decide what is *feeling good* for you, like I have decided what is a good time for me.

My full job description is to help you discover that from now on all *misery is optional* and to uncover in you the skills that easily and deliberately create whatever you decide to call *feeling good*.

Now you know why I wrote this book.

CHAPTER 1

MISERY IS (Indeed!) OPTIONAL

Just twenty-five years ago our understanding of how thoughts create reality was in its infancy, and the notion of deliberate transformation of the self was but a beautiful dream. Today, we have the most powerful product for designer living available: *Primary Domino Thinking*. It has helped hundreds of people transform their lives and businesses, and achieve the future they always wanted but never could attain. Many have found that powerful and versatile *Primary Domino Thinking* can be effectively utilized anywhere, anytime, and for any deliberate transition one wishes to make in one's life. Why wait for circumstances to change you, when you can change circumstances?

Unlimited Power

Throughout human history, the brightest and best minds have attempted to discover how people can live better and have happier and more prosperous lives.

Famous scientists like Leonardo da Vinci, Albert Einstein and David Bohm attempted to achieve intellectual happiness by understanding the physical laws that bind us. They succeeded in creating some of the most powerful changes in all of human history.

Accomplished psychologists like Sigmund Freud, Abraham Maslow and Albert Ellis sought happiness through understanding the human mind and emotions, and their work has liberated many people from mental misery.

Autogenics, the famous visualization technique developed by the Germans, has significantly boosted the performance of athletes around the world for the last three decades. Reportedly, over 70% of the athletes in the 1996 Summer Olympics in Atlanta utilized some form of psychotechnology to increase their performance.

Can you imagine the combined power of all of these fields finally harnessed and utilized together? *Primary Domino Thinking* does exactly that. It is solidly built upon the findings of the most accomplished and recognized minds in history. *Primary Domino Thinking* is the end result of all this work, carefully interpreted, field-tested, refined and tested again many times, and then expressed in easy-to-understand language so it can work for everybody in their daily life.

The Latest Breakthrough: PRIMARY DOMINO THINKING

We are all seeking after the same basic goal in our every thought, word or action. Laborers, athletes, followers of religions, artists, misers, executives, and even addicts, the mentally ill, and those acting criminally, are all striving to overcome dissatisfaction and to *feel good* each in their own way.

One might say that all directed human energy, whether deemed respectable or not, has some form of *feeling good* as its goal. Usually the source for our *feeling good* is sought "out there" somewhere. This drives us to worry and scheme in order to exert some control over those "out there" things and people in order to ensure a continuous supply of our *feeling good* prescriptions.

Because they were also "out there" oriented, many of the great seekers have missed the critical point that what we really need is to be *our own self-contained supplier of feeling good.* For most of our existence we were encouraged to put our lives in the care of others, and it never dawned on us that we could provide the requirements for feeling good to ourselves without assistance from any "out there" person, event, or thing.

The purpose of this book is to help you rise from the ashes of this old-fashioned, inaccurate, and often destructive belief and to place you and/or your business in the pilot's seat of your life in ways you never dreamed possible, simply by utilizing *Primary Domino Thinking.*

Primary Domino Thinking is easy to use and the results will be surprisingly fast and effective. It not only works, but it can be fun too. It is the most powerful way ever developed to put you in control of who you are now, and who you choose to become in the future. You will experience more assurance and success than ever before because you will now have a method that will work for you anytime anywhere.

CHAPTER 2

EVERY THOUGHT HAS POWER

The Power of Thought

Every single thought has power. Each thought you had in the past contributed to your being exactly what and where you are right now. Every thought you have from now on will determine what and where you - personally or professionally - will be in the future.

Always remember: Some thoughts are more powerful than others, and some are more powerful still, but they ALL have power.

- Thomas Alva Edison had the thought of running electricity across a wire in a glass globe, and lit up the world.

- Mr. Sears and Mr. Roebuck had the thought of selling clothes through a catalog, and became two of the world's most famous merchants.

- King Gillette's multi-million dollar safety razor empire arose from a single thought.

- Walter Lantz's million dollar success with the cartoon character Woody Woodpecker came from a single thought evoked from an event on his honeymoon with his wife (who, by the trivia way, became the voice of Woody).
- Cures for diseases, which saved many thousands of lives, started with just a single thought from historical figures such as Pasteur, Lister, Salk, and Sabine.

If a single thought can change our world, then certainly the right single thought can change your life or business for the better. The *Primary Domino Thinking* process makes what happened by accident for these now famous people happen deliberately for you.

The Secret

There is a secret to joining the happy few and escaping the dull grind that plagues so many. Successful people know how to think in a certain way. They know that by putting effort into certain patterns of thought they create magical outcomes in their lives. They know that the right form of thought puts them in the driver's seat of their lives, able to obtain all they desire. Now *you* will know. You will never have to fall further and further behind in this life, left with only unfulfilled dreams, frustrated wishes and deep regrets.

THE FIRST CLUE:

Action brings about results, but all action is preceded by particular thoughts. If we know the right thoughts, the right actions come about automatically along with the desired results.

Your Real Source of Power

The power that propels your life comes from inside YOU. You might believe that power comes through you from some mystical source, but even then it must inevitably reside within you in order to be utilized. There is no reason for *Primary Domino Thinking* to conflict with your personal spirituality. It does not interfere with any interpretation of a higher power.

Even if you firmly believe that God is geographically located "out there" somewhere, God must still manifest within you to be effective. This concept of power location is not unlike the fact that sunshine or nutrients must eventually be internalized by you if they are to benefit you.

By all means, continue to hold the spiritual beliefs you currently hold, and utilize this manual in becoming even more effective in that faith. *Primary Domino Thinking* is designed to empower anyone who has the ability to think about thinking and, therefore, is respectful of all faiths (or lacks of faith).

THE SECOND CLUE:

You can fight ownership of and responsibility for your life as long as you wish, but eventually you will discover there simply is no other healthy choice.

To Be Truly Free

Some people believe that what you are about to learn is strange. Some believe that individuals do not have the ability to consciously determine their own lives. These beliefs are usually the result of childhood "recordings" that were programmed into us by authority figures. Those "big people" ran our lives when we were little, and at that time it was smart for us to believe in everything they said and did.

To be truly free in our lives today we must rise above unnecessary, restrictive and outdated recordings in our heads. They no longer serve us well, and in fact, are like shackles that keep us from having everything we want and deserve in this life. I am talking about negative voices from the past in your head that tell you that "Nothing will work for me" or " I am ugly" or "Life is crap" etc.

We could spend a lot of time analyzing why those tape-making authority figures believed in the philosophy of restriction. We could even get into blaming them for our shortcomings today. Or we could defend or justify why they did what they did. But do you really want to spend more of your precious life time on people who restricted you?

THE THIRD CLUE:

It is your right, your destiny, and your obligation to joyfully develop your ultimate knowledge and power.

You were given the abilities to develop yourself to your optimal potential (and just wait until you find out how *optimal* it really is!). What a crime against yourself not to do that. What a crime of neglect against others to deny them the benefit of associating with you as your maximally developed powerful, wise, loving, sensitive, and strong human self!

The Seven Paralyzing Fears

Fear of physical pain is natural. Pay attention to warnings about physical danger, since they are life preservers: "Buckle Up!" "Watch for Falling Rocks!" "Caution - Dangerous Curve" and, "Look Both Ways!"

It is also normal to have fear in other situations not involving danger of physical pain. This type of fear is called *anxiety*, and it is very prevalent in our lives today. The end result of anxiety is that we become paralyzed by the mere anticipation of any of the following:

- The fear of making a mistake
- The fear of being criticized
- The fear of losing someone's affection

- The fear of appearing foolish or insane
- The fear of disturbing established habits or traditions
- The fear of being excluded or ostracized
- The fear of realizing our true identity

The first six fears boil down to a negative outlook based on the thought, "I don't want to be wrong." It doesn't take rocket scientist thinking to deduce why you grew up with such an aversion to being wrong; BUT just in case you need a little reminder, here they are from A-Z:

When you were "wrong" you may have been:
a) physically punished
b) called "silly" or "stupid"
c) made fun of
d) frowned at
e) denied privileges or food
f) shunned
g) denied affection
h) shamed
i) guilted out
j) laughed at
k) intimidated
l) given a low grade
m) molested

n) criticized

o) yelled at

p) made to feel insane

q) humiliated

r) sent away

s) threatened with horrible consequences (I'll skin you alive/I wish you were dead/Wait'll your father comes home/You'll roast in hell)

t) told you were evil/bad/sinful/a devil or demon

u) told you would be the death of your parent

v) isolated in a room/closet/basement/car

w)threatened with an object (belt/stick/switch club/hand/paddle/knife/gun/etc.)

x) given an increased workload

y) grounded

z) threatened with a loss of credibility and/or status

Do any of these affect you while reading them? Well, of course, they do. We carry these with us into adulthood and they resonate in our very tissues when we anticipate making a mistake. *They also resonate when we anticipate trying something new*, and this can keep us from developing our full potential in person or profession. What a crime against ourselves to let these old recordings limit us today. When you wish to grow and cannot, it creates a toxic internal environment of frustration and resentment.

To counteract this: When those old limiting recordings start increasing in volume in your head as you anticipate trying something new, replace them with this one: **"Stop! I am *learning* right now!"**

"A man learns to ice skate by staggering around making a fool of himself. Indeed, we progress in all things by resolutely making fools of ourselves." - George Bernard Shaw

The Seventh Fear

The fear of realizing our true identity is a bit complex. We are basically not who we usually think we are. Within the human is incredible power, incredible intelligence, and incredible passion - including the passion of all the emotions...especially joy. But how often do you fully experience your "true self"? How often do you feel super powerful, super intelligent, and super joyous? My experience is that people are so conditioned to being filled with worry, doubt, and powerlessness, that they have come to see these false states as daily reality! They buy the delusion to the extent that they have developed an actual fear of their true identity. Perhaps Sigmund Freud said it best:

"The cause of most psychological illness is the fear of knowledge of oneself - of one's emotions, impulses, memories, capacities, potentialities, and of one's destiny."

Is it possible that all along we have been capable of making all of our dreams come true, but didn't know it? How could this happen? Again, one way it happened was that we were "seduced" into believing that our source of power was "out there," when indeed it was not. We have continued to look for happiness and satisfaction by grasping at "out there" things, only to find them temporarily satisfying at best.

THE FOURTH CLUE:

If what you want is not what you need you will never get enough.

We grasped at apparitions, and grasped for more when those did not satisfy us. Perhaps we were looking in the wrong direction. Grasping for and receiving another paycheck, another compliment, another tidbit of food, another knickknack, another relationship, has never held us for long, has it? There has been that nagging feeling that something was missing, or that things were just a little too precarious, or superfluous, or hollow.

Perhaps you have felt that you didn't know who you were...and at the same time you were afraid of knowing your real self. That is the 7th fear. You are more powerful than you ever realized, and the fear you may have experienced in becoming your true self is usually a mixture of confusion and awe from that potential power.

You are entitled to immense power because your destiny is not to wait on handouts, or run from one tidbit to the next, or to constantly worry whether or not life will take care of you. You have a much grander purpose. *Primary Domino Thinking* will give you bountiful tools to deal with any fear you might have as you move along the path of empowerment. Keep your chin up, keep reading and working through this book, and remember:

Courage in your personal or professional life is not fearlessness. Courage is going on despite fear.

You already have courage. You have demonstrated this many times in your life. Remember? Maybe it was the first swim in deep water. Or the first jump off the high dive. Or the driver's test. Or the job interview. Or the shot you had to get. Or the tooth you let the dentist drill. You HAVE gone on despite the fear many times. Just because you are anxious or afraid is no reason to stop reaching for what you want or need, is it?

CHAPTER 3

PRIMARY DOMINO THINKING EXPLAINED

The Nine Principles ofPrimary Domino Thinking

Primary Domino Thinking is the most powerful new method for improving your life that has ever existed. It represents a dynamic and powerful blend of psychology-technology that I developed and field-tested for over 10 years.

As a psychotherapist and consultant, I found that many people wanted to change their lives for the better permanently. "I have tried everything," said a client. "Exercise, self-talk, meditation; they all seemed to work for about a month or less. Nothing ever made a permanent difference in my life."

I have heard the same complaint from so many people. There are many ideas and programs, but none that seem to make a permanent difference. Is something being overlooked, I wondered? It had to be possible for people to have *the ability to permanently change their lives for the better at will without depending continually on sources of power outside themselves.*

It was from this thought that I hit on the concept of *Primary Domino Thinking*. How appropriate that the conception of the field came from but a single thought! But when you think about it, each of us probably started with a single thought. Whether it was a "glint in your daddy's eye" or your parents making a conscious decision to have a child, look what has happened as a result of *that* single thought!

[For the curious reader, the history and in-depth explanation of the development of *Primary Domino Thinking*, including case studies, can be found in my previous book, *PHOENIX FLIGHT MANUAL... Rising Above the Ashes of Ordinary Existence*, Three Blue Herons Publishing, Inc.]

This angle of vision is the same angle necessary to look at the potential for bringing about change in our lives and businesses. With a single thought you can move mountains, if you happen to be in a mountain-moving mood! The thought does not move the mountain. The first thought sets other thoughts in motion much like the first domino in a chain reaction of dominoes. Just any haphazard thought will not get the mountain moved, unless you're very lucky. *The specifications of the first thought are critical, if the thought is to have the results you desire.*

This is the foundation of *Primary Domino Thinking* - a well-structured primary thought that can create magic in your personal or professional life.

Principles are the *assumptions* behind any endeavor. There are nine simple principles that underlie Primary Domino Thinking.

The Nine Principles of Primary Domino Thinking

1. People have the ability to think and do.

2. People have the ability to grow and develop.

3. People can change outcomes through decision-making.

4. All human change begins with a primary thought.

5. People can decide at any moment to switch from being directed by others and circumstances to being self-directed.

6. Individual experience is one's reality, and is subjectively interpreted, validated and displayed.

7. People can modify the impact that their personal history has upon themselves.

8. People are best served by elegant honesty and integrity.

9. Humans are spiritual beings, and are more than the apparent sum of their parts.

Note: It is important for you to read the explanations of the following principles. Much of the essential knowledge base for your success is wrapped up in them.

The First Principle:

People have the ability to think and do.

Everyone has within themselves the ability to think of something and then do it. The thought precedes the action. Have you ever turned on the television or bought something without first having the thought to do it? Thoughts are so natural that we may not be aware of them. By the time we reach adulthood, many of our actions (for example, walking and talking) are instinctive and seemingly without thought.

We are not always consciously aware of our thoughts, but aware or not, each thought is registered in the chemistry and electricity of our brains. The registered thought can then act to produce a result. This is how the human brain and body work today, and how they always have.

Not much has changed about how the mind and body function, but how we utilize those functions certainly has changed. At one time scientists such as James Watson and B. F. Skinner believed humans were merely a series of habituated reflex actions, much like the automatic behavior that happens to your leg when the doctor hits your knee with that nasty little hammer. Today we know that we have capabilities other than just responding. We have the ability to think about what we are going to do before we do it. More importantly, we have learned that we can think about our thoughts, and even *choose* the type of thinking we will do. The lingo for this is *metacognition*, being consciously aware about our thinking. This ability is what makes the human being so remarkable and powerful!

The Second Principle:

People have the ability to grow and develop.

Once you were an infant. Then it was time to go to kindergarten. There were other schools after that, but even after you left school, you were still learning, developing and growing. Many of us are very surprised just how much we learned in our 20's. We were surprised because schools, friends and elders kept talking about "when you grow up" as if it was a final stage. The implication was that once you reached 18 or 21 or graduated from college, etc., you would be "done" with all that growing and stretching stuff. What a surprise to find out that graduation was a beginning more than it was an ending!

Today there are many courses in colleges on adult development, and in those courses it is common knowledge that adults have stages of development just as children do. Students of human development discover that a person never stops developing unless they choose to stop; that our potential as human beings is endless.

It is the natural order of things for us to constantly be learning and stretching our capabilities. *Could it be that many people are unhappy today because they have forgotten how to grow, or have locked themselves into places in their lives where they feel they are unable to develop?* It makes us unhappy to be restrained, kept from our destiny, and from tapping into the wonderful vitality of the growing processes that it takes to get us there!

The Third Principle:

People can change outcomes through decision-making.

People make decisions and change their outcomes all the time. Shall I go to the movies? Yes. And the outcome of my evening is different than if I had said "No." Shall I get drunk until I am sick? No, I will only have two beers. And the outcome is different. Shall I buy this dress or put the money in savings? Whichever I decide, the outcome will be decided as well.

All day long we face one fork in the road of our lives after another. Whichever fork we decide to choose will determine the outcomes in our lives. It is easy, although painful sometimes, to see this retrospectively. Almost as if viewing an old roadmap, we can look back and see where we made major differences in our lives just by one simple decision. I know a fellow who mailed inquiries to every branch of the service on the same day and decided that he would join the one who replied first. It was the Marines. His life has been different to this day because of that one capricious decision. Who you decided to associate with, how you spent your money, where you decided to live, etc., all brought you to where you are today. This same pattern will continue into your future.

The Fourth Principle:

All human change begins with a primary thought.

Have you ever attempted to determine how you arrived at a certain topic in a conversation? Did you begin to backtrack to find the source of the thinking - to find the "seed" thought that started it all? Remember the feeling when you found it? It was funny, wasn't it? You marveled at how all those ideas and conversation and emotions flowed from just one thought.

Several years ago a fellow made a lot of guest appearances at malls and on television. He would set up huge displays of dominoes, some that covered an area as large as a gymnasium floor. The dominoes spelled out words, or made pictures or portraits. Some dominoes were colored to create beautiful patterns, some climbed miniature staircases, and some swung like Tarzan on little ropes when they were struck. Days were spent setting up the elaborate demonstration. As the time drew near, so did the crowds and cameras. The anticipation was exhilarating. A hush would fall over the crowd before the fellow would finally step forward and, with a flourish, initiate the whole display by starting a single domino falling in a certain direction. What followed was extraordinary. People laughed, cheered and applauded at the beauty and intricacy of....what? *Connections*. Connections that created marvelous patterns...all beginning with a PRIMARY DOMINO.

Our thought patterns each begin with a single thought, and they create a marvelous display, known as *our life*. Each single thought we have can spin off into many areas of thought with the behaviors that may follow. Thoughts can also just dead-end and go nowhere, or even be circular, like a dog chasing its tail, and go nowhere in a hurry. But know these very important fundamental truths about thought:

- **Every single thought has some power.**

- **Each one you had in the past contributed to your being exactly what and where you are right now.** (No, it wasn't fate, luck, or coincidence.)

- **Every single thought you have from now on will determine what and where you will be in the near and distant future.**

- **Some thoughts are more powerful than others...and some are more powerful still.**

It becomes obvious that it can be of tremendous benefit to pay attention to our thoughts, especially those we endow with Primary Domino power. This book will teach you how.

The Fifth Principle:
People can decide at any moment to switch from being directed by others and/or circumstances to being self-directed.

We were born small and dependent. Everybody around us was bigger, stronger and more experienced. We let others direct our lives a great deal. Eventually we learned to direct our own lives some of the time. Today we can decide when we want to let others (or circumstances) direct us, or when we want to decide for ourselves.

The Sixth Principle:

Individual experience is one's reality, and is subjectively interpreted, validated and displayed.

For centuries humans have contemplated the question, "What *is* "reality"? People have come up with many, many theoretical answers. This should not be a difficult issue! Let's just talk about what we *know*. We *know* we have experiences. We *know* experiences are real to *us*. We *know* that people don't always see things the same way. We know the way people see things is the way they experience them, therefor, that's their "reality."

This is why we argue: we are trying to force someone to see an experience *our* way. What we are saying in an argument is, "My reality is better than yours." This is, of course, rarely the case. Everyone's reality seems well-suited to them if you are willing to step back and take an objective look at each individual's life. But who has the time, inclination, or expertise to perform a case study on each person with whom you disagree? It is easier and more elegant for you to accept the following as a motto: *Just because you and I disagree doesn't mean one of us is wrong.*

> Circumstances do not create a person, they reflect a person.
> - James Allen
>
> This is a rather shattering statement, is it not? If you will make just this belief part of your life, things will begin to change for you. It is a very significant Primary Domino Thought of understanding and personal liberation and personal and/or professional growth.

The Seventh Principle:

People can modify the impact that their personal history has upon themselves.

You have already done this many times. We have all received new information or a new angle of vision regarding a past event that has changed the impact of the original event upon us. A client once came to me angry about his dysfunctional family upbringing. He felt he had been neglected and abandoned. He had to grow up basically on his own.

I helped this client feel his anger, which he certainly had a right to, because every child deserves a loving, nurturing home. But then one day he realized it was the desertion in his childhood that had helped him develop the skills needed to start, run and prosper in his own business. It was his *resentment* about his childhood that was raining on his parade, not his actual past experiences. With that realization he permanently shifted his feelings from unfinished anger to gratitude for the gifts those circumstances gave him. His history was changed, and after all those years!

Shorter versions of this happen to us all the time. Another client was going to a prayer meeting with three of her friends when her car stalled and drifted to the side of the highway. Angry at her old car, and upset that she couldn't get it to start, she and her friends decided to wait for the highway patrol. After 20 minutes and no police, she decided to try starting the car again, and it did! Proceeding around the next curve on the highway she found her highway patrolman. He was busy stopping traffic because of a huge accident which had occurred 30 minutes before involving many cars causing many serious injuries! The car stalling had obviously been a blessing in disguise. Had it not stalled they may well have been involved in the accident.

> *No matter what happens to me, I am going to benefit from it one way or another.*

Often we look back on events in our lives and realize they were for the best, although we ranted and raved at the time. Wouldn't you like the ability to know events are for the best as they occur, instead of waiting for it to *maybe* dawn on you *someday*? Imagine the feeling of knowing instant gratitude for whatever happens in your life! Imagine internalizing this belief:

With that mindset, and without taking away your privilege of protesting wrongdoing, you always win no matter what happens!

The Eighth Principle:

People are best served by elegant honesty and integrity.

Primary Domino Thinking is about truth - the liberating type of truth. And it is about power - the liberating type of power. It is about freeing people to design their own lives in the way they see fit. It is a vehicle to get you to wherever you want to be in your life. Automobiles make a great metaphor for this power: Some people use them responsibly to get from one place to another more efficiently, and some misuse automobiles and create harm for themselves and others.

Although people do gain things through dishonesty, it is only because they have never felt the power of the deeper truths of the human being. In reality they have settled for less, because what they achieved through dishonest means is a drop in the bucket compared to what they could have had by applying those same energies honestly.

It is important to use elegant (as opposed to "brutal") honesty and honorable intentions in applications of your newly acquired power. You may make errors in judgement with *Primary Domino Thinking*, but they will be honest mistakes and will, therefore, benefit you. On the other hand, misusing power towards unscrupulous ends is not a prerogative. It is important to respect yourself and others as well as the process.

There is no need not to, since you can have anything you want faster and better the honest and elegant way once you learn to utilize *Primary Domino Thinking.*

The Ninth Principle:
Humans are spiritual beings, and are more than the apparent sum of their parts.

You are not just a bunch of tissue that happens to think. You are more than an accumulation of reflexes that happens to move. People have much higher levels of possible existence than these open to them. Some have experienced it and *know* this to be true. Others surmise or hope it is true. *It is true.* Many have risen above their history, their circumstances, and their ailments to prosper in this lifetime. They did it through tapping into that part of themselves that is difficult to describe, but is, nonetheless, real - that invisible part of you that gives meaning, sustenance and vitality to life.

CHAPTER 4

TAKE CHARGE OF YOUR LIFE

If you are not aware that you are in control of your life, it is understandable. Your first experiences with control were when you were born. And since you were born small and dependent, you had very little ability to control anything. Everyone in your universe was bigger, more experienced, and seemed to know more than you did about everything. Sometimes they convinced you of this with love. Sometimes they convinced you of this with fear, or even pain. They even convinced you that they knew what you needed: "Eat this; it's good for you." "Do this, or you will be sorry." "Do that, or you'll get sick." No wonder we grew up with a tendency to trust other people's judgements more than our own!

As adults it can still be confusing and difficult to know when we should listen to others and when we should be our own boss.

CLUE:

Part A -

You are the resident expert on **what** *your needs are.*

Part B -

You have the right to determine **how** *your needs will be met.*

Being told what your needs are teaches you not to develop a trust in your own internal sense of what is best and true for you. When this is done to you, it has very disempowering effects. The erroneous thought that you don't know what is best for yourself becomes entrenched in your consciousness long before you know you have a choice about it. At the time it was wise to go along with the program since the authority figures implanting this erroneous thought were also the all-important keepers of the food and the affection. Often the needs they convinced us were our own, were actually their needs.

Believing that we didn't know what was best for us was our first sellout on ourselves. Since then we have been told so many times what to do, how to do it, how not to do it and what we needed, that we have forgotten one very important thing: Nobody, but nobody, is supposed to know what we need better than we do.

Our choices today consist mostly of going along with what we were convinced of in our early years. The major thought that controlled us then and still can today is: *"If you don't _____ then bad things will happen."* If you don't do what Dad says he will punish you. If you don't do what Mom says, you will get a frown. If you don't do what teacher says, you will get an F. If you don't eat your meat, you can't have any pudding. If you don't do what the supervisor wants, you won't get a raise. If you continue in this fashion, I won't love you or will even abandon you.

Unfortunately, no one ever served notice to our subconscious mind that childhood was over! No one officially declared that we could stop being threatened and seduced into buying this erroneous notion that we don't know what is best for us. So let's make it official:

> *You, and only you, are supposed to be in charge of your life. Only you can truly know your needs and act or not act on them. Your life can only be lived by you.*

This will make life much easier and much, much more fun, and healthier too! You will no longer feel manipulated by others, or as if you are living life from a "have to" posture, i.e. no more resentments towards anyone or anything (except yourself when you refuse to use your new tools and skills!).

Primary Domino Thinking is designed to help you get comfortable with and efficient in running your own life. Think of this book as a friendly hand on the rear fender of your bike after the training wheels have been removed! At first it may be uncomfortable. The power you will possess may seem dizzying. The responsibility may appear overwhelming. The uncertainty resident in any new endeavor can be anxiety-producing, like riding the bike without the training wheels for the first time. Remember: It is supposed to feel uncomfortable, anxiety-producing, or even dizzying at first. This is a natural response to change. **This is just temporary**.

Your Locus of Control

Locus comes from the Latin word for *place*. In a human, *locus of control* denotes where the source of one's power is felt to be located. If you have an **internal** locus of control you see a high correlation between your choices and the outcomes in your life. If you have an **external** locus of control, you see little correlation between your choices and the outcomes in your life.

External Locus of Control	Internal Locus of Control
Empowerment ======>	
Victim; irresponsible;	Empowered; responsible;
Unhealthy and dependent;	Healthy;
Little ability to do anything	Ability to make good
but suffer/hope or wait on	things occur and fully
handouts.	enjoy the results.

Empowerment is the process of moving from an external locus of control to an internal locus of control. It is the evolution of a person's potential to deliberately design his/her world - personally OR professionally.

Limits and Boundaries

Make it one of your goals to realize you have an *internal locus of control*, because the truth is, you really do! You establish your locus of control best by deliberately choosing to set healthy *limits* and *boundaries*.

Limits are how far you will let yourself go (in dealing with yourself).

Boundaries are how far you will let other people go (in their dealings with you).

Examples of *limits*:

"I am going to walk two miles today."

"I will do the dishes later."

"I will refrain from using profanity."

"I will not call Bill today."

"I am going to eat under 2200 calories today."

"I will rest and relax all day Sunday."

"I will obey the Scout Law."

A reminder about limits: If you continue to set limits and break them you get weaker. Set limits that are easy on you on at first so you can build strength and confidence.

Examples of *boundaries*:

"You can't talk to me that way."

"No, you cannot borrow $5, because you never repay me when you say you will."

"You can touch me, but you can't touch me like that."

"You kids will have to fix your own lunch today."

"I won't tolerate degrading sexual innuendos from you."

"Please don't call me anymore."

"Please don't let your dog come into my yard."

A reminder about boundaries: If boundaries are to be effective they must have *consequences* if they are violated. You may not need to announce consequences in advance, but YOU need to know what they are. Do not set boundaries if you are not willing to follow through firmly on the consequences.

Power

Personal power is an odd thing. If you believe you have it, you do, and if you believe you don't, you don't! Most people wish they had more power, but almost everyone fails to realize where the source of that power is located. The result is that remains hidden and is, therefore, unavailable!

CLUE:

All of your power comes from within.

You do not have to go anywhere, or to anyone, or buy anything, to have more power; you already have it! Your issue with power is not finding it, but in effectively using what you already have. In other words, it is a *delusion* (an untruth that is believed to be true) that you are powerless. Humans with an external locus of control are living a delusional existence...no wonder they feel so anxious!

This clue does make gaining empowerment a lot easier than if you had to locate power somewhere "out there." You must, however, be willing to uncover the power you do have. It seems like this would be an obvious and easy decision for most people to make but there are several reasons why it is not.

Six Excuses for Staying Powerless

1) If I don't have power, I don't have to be responsible.

2) If I don't have power, it's not *my* fault when things don't work out.

3) It takes too much effort/initiative to use power.

4) People expect a lot from you when you have power.

5) If you have power, some people won't like you or will try to take it away.

6) "Good" people/Christians/citizens/followers/etc. shouldn't have too much power.

And, of course, these are all true for you if you believe them to be true. They are not The Truth.They are just true for you because you believe them to be so. It is much more to your advantage to believe inobjective truthabout power. You will benefit healthfully along with everyone who comes in contact with you. Since the powerless route is one filled with ignorance, poor health, frustration, negativity, fear and other unfunny things, it is important to clearly refute the excuses for staying powerless.

1) If I don't have power, I don't have to be responsible.

You have been responsible for how you interact with life since you were conceived (and, who knows, maybe even before!). No one can get into your skin and decide how to deal or not deal with life, because that skin is already occupied by **you**. All your wishes and arguments to the contrary won't change this simple fact.

I met a worn-out looking middle-aged woman in a laundromat on a Sunday afternoon folding a big stack of men's jeans.

"Great way to spend a sunny afternoon, isn't it?" I quipped.

She sighed, "Yes, if I could get these boys to live on their own I wouldn't have to be here."

"How old are your boys?" I asked.

"23 and 27." She replied, "They both work construction, and still live at home."

"Why don't you ask them to live on their own?" I, perhaps impertinently, replied.

She sighed again, "Boy, that would be nice, but how can I do that?"

"Well, you could start by slipping a note into those jeans saying, 'Enjoy these clean jeans, guys, because they are the last ones I'm doing.' Then you could do the same with the lunch box I suspect you prepare for them every day: 'Enjoy this lunch, boys, because it's the last one I'm preparing.' If they don't get the hint, then put a note on their pillow saying, 'Enjoy this bed tonight...' "

She sighed again (something, I was beginning to suspect, she did a lot of), "That would be so nice, but how do I do that?"

This woman could not see that she was choosing to remain powerless so she wouldn't have to be responsible for throwing out her grown, but still dependent, men-kids. Notice how this shirking of responsibility doesn't change the amount of work that still has to be done? In this case it appeared the woman was actually working harder at something she didn't want to do by refusing the apparent "burden" of responsibility. How ironic - and how sad.

2) If I don't have power, it's not my fault when things don't work out.

Sure it is. If you gave up your responsibility (power), you share the blame *whether you admit it or not*. If you didn't actually cause woundings or problems, you still share in the responsibility for the healing and solving. And, by the way, why worry so much about "fault"? If it actually was your fault when something went wrong, it's O.K.; you aren't supposed to be perfect...or hadn't you noticed?

A client said in session one day, "My son Derek is so unhappy. His father insists on his going to law school, and Derek wants to be a teacher. I just hate to see him hurting like this. I think he should be allowed to follow his dream of teaching."

"Why can't he?" I asked.

"Because his father pays the tuition, and that's what he wants." "Have you spoken up on this?" I asked.

"I can't really, Harry earns the money and he is paying Derek's tuition. I just hope he's happy when Derek is miserable, or even flunks out."

"But aren't you going to hurt if Derek hurts?"

"Yes, I'm his Mother, of course I will hurt. But it won't be my fault."

My client won't speak her mind just so she won't have to assume responsibility, even though she knows people, including herself, are going to be in pain. Chances are the pain she is saving by shirking her responsibility will not even come close to the pain she will experience for a long time to come, not to mention Derek's pain. It *is* her fault that she did not assume the responsibility she should have assumed in these circumstances.

3) It takes too much effort/initiative to use power.

You are actually expending the same amount of effort no matter what you are doing...watching television or working in the garden or writing a letter or jogging. Life energy is not measured in calorie expenditure, but is a very personal investment we call "time." In other words, it takes just as much "time" to watch an hour of television as it does to work in the garden for an hour, etc. What is really operating in this excuse for staying powerless is the uneasiness caused by moving outside your *comfort zone* (which we will examine closely in the next chapter).

Effort is not the issue at all. In reality, it takes extra energy to suppress effort, since our molecules are in constant motion and are naturally inclined to be doing things all the time.

I see in people the effects of not maintaining their health through proper physical exercise. Their response is that it just takes too much energy and time. "I am already tired," they say, "I wouldn't have any energy at all if I worked out!" I'm going to ask you, the reader, to refute this for yourself. Ask five people who work out regularly if they have more or less energy because they exercise. I guarantee that they will say, to a person, that they have *more* energy because they exercise. And while you have them buttonholed, ask them this question: "How do you find the time to exercise?" They will tell you explicitly.

Time and energy are actually elastic. It is your mind that is not. *Primary Domino Thinking* will fix that!

4) People expect a lot from you when you have power.

Like they don't when you don't! People expect a lot from people on welfare as well as people like Bill Gates. Expectations from others are a constant. This incorrect belief is a worrisome carryover from childhood when people were always holding up a high bar and expecting you to jump over it. "You can do better than that!" "Why aren't you as good as Brad/Tina/Soo/Dancing Light?" Expectations are usually critical in nature.

Expectations are like handcuffs; they measure you against outcomes. And, of course, you always come up short. It's the nature of the beast. No one speaks of expectations if something has already been accomplished! Expectations are only mentioned when there is a perceived shortfall.

We must be aware of expectations of others, the world, and especially of ourselves, that we do not create and sustain a prison of our own making.

Goals, however, are different and very important. They give direction, meaning and a sense of accomplishment.

The deadening question is, "What do they expect of me?"

The liberating question is, "What is my Purpose, and what can help me accomplish it?"

It is very intelligent to consider your Purpose whenever you are about to invest your resources (time, $, energy, self) in order to align yourself in the most healthfully, powerful manner.

5) If you have power, some people won't like you or will try to take it away.

People are hungry for and scared of power at the same time; i.e., it is very attractive. People want power so they can solve all their problems and get what they want. People are afraid of it because they have seen what Hitler-types, military leaders, politicians, criminals, and angry parents have done with it. People are also afraid of the "feeling" of power because it is a very heady experience, and they are simply not familiar with it. Trust this: It's a feeling you can get used to! You will, of course, need to learn to wisely use your power with those drawn to you.

6) "Good" people/Christians/citizens/followers/etc., shouldn't have power.

Yeah, right. This is a ruse perpetuated by powerless people who don't know how to be otherwise. If there is one thing every great leader (including religious ones) possessed, it was power. How can you truly do "good deeds" without power? With no power you can just barely benefit yourself and will, of necessity, be totally occupied with doing just that. You will also drain those you are forced to rely upon. This planet of ours is facing some major crises. It needs powerful people to help preserve resources, not powerless people to drain them.

I remember a client being in constant emotional pain due to her marriage to an addictive spouse. Her usual statement to herself was a big sigh followed by, "If it's God's will, he will straighten up someday."

In other words, she was saying: "It's not up to me to do anything about my life. Let God do it." I reminded her that God had given her a brain and willpower to utilize in solving these things for herself.

Some people try to have power over others by remaining helpless. These people don't know any other way to get their needs met. Their self-sufficiency tools and skills are dormant. But, no one wants to feel like a leech. *Primary Domino Thinking* is the total opposite of "leechdom."

To summarize: You are accountable for your power. If you misuse your power, you are accountable. If you remain powerless, you are accountable for that as well. This applies in your personal life and in your professional life - whether you own your business or work for someone else.

CHAPTER 5

THE COMFORT ZONE

Have you ever wondered what keeps you from changing? What prevents you from just dropping certain thoughts, words or behaviors in the wink of an eye, and then picking up brand new ones? Think about the delight in having the kind of personal power that would enable you to choose to be a non-smoker, or detach from a destructive relationship, or instantly change your mood from anxiety to euphoria. Imagine making any of those things happen simply and quickly! Why can't we? What keeps us stuck in old patterns we either don't or shouldn't want any more? Why do we feel so anxious, reluctant or incapable of changing at will?

Our love-hate relationship with ruts

Your comfort zone runs your life! Think about the implications of this statement! Your comfort zone is your personal space of behaviors (thoughts/words/actions) in which you feel comfortable. Needless to say, many of the behaviors with which you are "comfy" are not beneficial for you in the long run! It's comfortable to continue eating potato chips (which can be 50% oil). It's comfortable to continue smoking cigarettes (cancer sticks). It's comfortable to not get exercise when you need it (the couch potato syndrome). We love our ruts even if we hate what they do to us.

Usually when we think of comfort, external things come to mind such as clothes, furniture, temperature, companions. But much more pertinent to the purposes of *Primary Domino Thinking* is the comfort zone each person carries *inside* them. Without an understanding of the internal comfort zone, personal growth and change will happen only against the greatest of resistance, if it happens at all.

The source of all conflict

Comfort zones and the accompanying warning signs they provide are different for every person. They are mostly a product of our culture, family and childhood experiences. We all have *learned* emotional signals that blare at us "You are now leaving your comfort zone!" sounding and feeling very much as if a Klingon vessel has uncloaked in our front yard.

Think how invested we are in our own zone of comfort. Realize that others are just as invested in theirs. Discrepancies in comfort zones are undoubtedly the source of most arguments. When people disagree, it is mostly their respective comfort zones arguing with each other. This is at the root of all personal, social, industrial, cultural, religious, and international conflict.

Guess what? We can quickly become enlightened in our relationships with others if we will allow ourselves to know that it is natural that everyone's comfort zone is different. Because we each have different backgrounds, learned responses, ways of interpreting reality, etc., we are naturally going to possess comfort zones that are different from one another. What would really be very odd is if we all felt the same way about everything.

> *Just because we don't agree doesn't mean one of us is wrong.*

Know this: *We are only bothered by differences in others because we perceive those differences as threatening us to move outside our own comfort zone.* So, we seemingly have no choice but to make them wrong in order to validate the strong investment we have in our own comfort zone. BUT, we DO have a choice. Once again, if we could just internalize this:

Others have worked just as hard to build their comfort zone as you have worked to build yours. It's not your place to threaten theirs any more than you want your own threatened. You probably have enough to do maintaining or changing your own.

The nasty business of codependence

Making other people part of the thermostatic controls for your comfort zone is a grievous setup for anxiety, friction and resentment. The syndrome of *codependence* that has risen to social awareness recently is indicative of this very serious issue. I define it simply as *looking elsewhere*. In terms of a relationship this means basically *using* other people as a mandatory part of your self-esteem, entertainment, power-tripping, security, mission, identity, etc. As much as this might be part of your life right now, you don't want to keep it. Why? Because it leads to hell on earth. (Most mall bookstores have plenty of paperbacks on the subject, and I strongly urge you to avail yourself of lots of reading on this topic if it is pertinent to you...like SOON.)

At the root of codependence is an internal inability to set, once again, healthy *limits and boundaries*. Just remember that one of the rights you do *not* have in a democratic society is to utilize another human being as an indispensable gear in the machinery of your comfort zone!

Challenging the comfort zone

In order to make effective transitions in your personal or professional life, there must be a willingness to challenge your comfort zone. Learn to be comfortable with the idea that sometimes you must temporarily experience discomfort in order to replace the old restrictive comfort zone with a new and more rewarding one. *Primary Domino Thinking* will make this much easier for you to do. Here are some signals that you are nearing the edges of your comfort zone.

Most frequent signals:

FEAR: at the root of this emotion is anticipation of losing something
ANGER: at the root of this emotion is fear; again, the anticipation of losing something
SADNESS: at the root of this emotion is the loss of something

Notice these ALL have to do with losing something. It does, of course, make sense to have feelings of loss when giving something up, but it doesn't make as much sense if you are going to gain something better than what you had. The purpose of *Primary Domino Thinking* is to always *trade-up*. You never wind up worse than you started. You always end up better. You will learn this as you use *PDT* more and more and your comfort zone alarms diminish and are replaced by eagerness and confidence.

Other signals that might show up:

GUILT (before you do anything):At the root of this is the knowledge that by trying something new you might make a mistake. This form of guilt-pain is prepayment in case you do.

DISCOURAGEMENT: The root of this feeling is lack of confidence in one's self and lack of belief that good effort produces good outcomes.

UNWORTHINESS: At the root of this feeling is a toxic crock of baloney based on the belief that one does not deserve better.

In a future chapter you will learn a breathing technique that will come in very handy when brushing up against the edges of your *comfort zone*. This will show you how flimsy the comfort zone boundaries are - you can just breathe through them!

CHAPTER 6

PRIMARY DOMINO THINKING

Primary Domino Thinking is the most powerful tool for self-actualization ever discovered. It is so powerful, that I have seen it succeed even for people who have never enjoyed success before.

Primary Domino Thinking is simple to understand, easy to use, and costs no more than the price of this book. With *PDT* you no longer need electronics, crystals, CDs, music, special surroundings or other people in order to succeed. It is the ultimate independent process. One merely needs knowledge of *Primary Domino Thinking* and a conscious mind for it to work. Sound like magic? It *is*...the natural magic you were born with taken to the ultimate realization of your potential.

The process of using *Primary Domino Thinking* moves you in the direction of supreme self-reliance. It uncovers potential powers you never knew existed inside you. It maximizes those powers like a ruby crystal does when transforming an ordinary ray of light into a powerful laser beam. *Primary Domino Thinking* can be quietly utilized anytime, anywhere, enhancing not only you, but everything and everyone around you!

Consciousness, experience and time

We may disagree on a lot of things, but the one thing we can agree on is that we have *experience*, or *consciousness* of our involvement in life. No matter where you have been locating your experience in the past, from now on know that it always happens inside you, in your consciousness. Try to imagine having an experience without being conscious of it! This is a very convenient truth for our purposes.

If all experience happens inside you, and you are the only one in there, then guess who is in charge? And, further, guess who can rearrange things if rearrangement is desired? You - and only you-can.

Secondly, not only is all experience inside of us, but it is also always happening right now, because experience can happen only in the present. As a matter of fact, most of us refer to our interior experiencing in terms of *time*. We need to discuss this thing we so blithely talk about called *time*, and I will make it quick:

There is no such thing as time. (Was that quick enough?)

Really, there is no such thing as time! It is just an agreed upon convenience, like a roadmap that represents Wisconsin. It isn't the *real* Wisconsin.

The map is a convenience in your trip across the state. It represents Wisconsin in order to facilitate your locating yourself *now*, where you have been in the *past* and where you are going in the *future* on your trip.

Our concept of time does the same thing, but *all* experience is, indeed, occurring in the NOW. There really is nothing else but NOW. *Past* and *future* are map-like conveniences of experience created in the NOW with your consciousness represented by *thinking*.

Your thinking creates your world - my thinking creates my world. Your thinking changes your world or keeps it the same. My thinking changes my world or keeps it the same. All consciousness-based power is in the NOW. It is a simple, but often overlooked, truth.

The Essential Five Steps of *PRIMARY DOMINO THINKING*

Primary Domino Thinking is a tool. It is a 5-step process designed to create self-determined improvements in your life. The transformations may be long-term, such as changing your finances, relationships, career, or body, or more short-term, such as changing your present mood, attitude or outlook. The transformations can be in your business, or could even be recreational, such as improving your golf or bowling score, batting average, or swimming skills.

It makes no difference what type of improvement is desired, the steps are the same. In order to utilize the *Primary Domino Thinking* one needs nothing more than knowledge of the 5-Steps and basically what you came into life with: Consciousness and Breath.

This is truly an independent tool, another reason why it is so empowering. It is you, with all your potential manifested. *Primary Domino Thinking* is the vehicle that moves you in the direction of supreme self-reliance. When you have mastered *Primary Domino*

Thinking, you will carry it conveniently and powerfully with you forever.

Primary Domino Thinking always works if utilized as prescribed. It is already in the most abbreviated form, so please use it exactly as described. When you understand that the *Primary Domino Thinking* can replace routines that people have spent years (or even a lifetime) utilizing in an attempt to improve their lives, then you begin to grasp the gravity of what you now hold in your hands.

THE FIVE STEPS OF *PRIMARY DOMINO THINKING*

STEP 1: Passionate Possession
To have impact, you must dare to get close.

STEP 2: Exploration of the Problem or Issue
Investigate the problem, discovering who truly owns it.

STEP 3: Producing the Primary Domino Thought
Generate your secret formula.

STEP 4: Primary Domino Thought Implantation
Apply your secret formula.

STEP 5: Regulation
Monitoring and adjusting makes the difference.

Each step will be thoroughly described in the following chapters. At the end of each chapter there will be space for you to work through a chosen issue of your own step by step as we go along. I heartily encourage you to take the time to do this.

> "If you cannot apply what you have learned,
> you have learned nothing."
>
> - John Dewey

How Primary Domino Thinking works

First, let's think backwards:

4) Any *outcome* in your life is a result of your behaviors (I wound up at the restaurant and had a good time.)

3) There were *behaviors that led to the outcome.* (I got dressed, pulled the car out of the garage and drove here, met my friends, ordered my food and had some conversation and laughs with my friends, thereby winding up at the restaurant and having a good time.)

2) The behaviors that led to the outcome were a result of your *thinking* (What should I wear? Red blouse? No. Too bright for the restaurant. Blue, maybe? Yes. Etc.etc.etc.etc.etc.etc.etc. Open the garage door. Back out carefully. Good. Etc.etc.etc. Turn right. Etc.etc.Turn left. Etc.etc.etc. Shall I meter park or use the parking garage? Hmmm, it could be a long lunch and I don't want to have to run out and plug the

meter - I might miss out on some great conversation - so I will use the parking garage. Turn left. Get a ticket. Which ramp? Etc.etc.etc.)

1) At the head of all those thoughts was a *Primary Domino Thought* that started everything falling into place. It is the most powerful thought in the bunch because once it was firmly *implanted* everything else happened almost automatically. (Hey, I think I will give Janet, Rosie and Jenni a call and see if they want to have some lunch. That would be fun!)

The 4th Principle of *PRIMARY DOMINO THINKING* states that **All human change begins with a primary thought**. To take this a step further, actually *all* outcomes are determined by *Primary Domino Thoughts*. The reason for this book is show you how to design a *PDT* that will create the outcomes you desire. The proper formation of the *Primary Domino Thought* and the effectiveness of its implantation always determines the outcomes in your life.

If you are experiencing chaos in your life it can always be traced back to subdued and random *Primary Domino Thoughts* that are created by chance, old recordings, habits, and/or lack of deliberation.

If your life keeps turning out like crap, then find the *Primary Domino Thoughts* buried at the bottom of the pile. They are always there. When you find them you will understand everything about the sewage in your life.

Again, the purpose of this book is to turn this around for you. Rather than being "victimized" by your old patterns, you can learn to deliberately implant the *Primary Domino Thoughts* that will transform your life automatically for the better.

The acronym of the 5-Steps of *Primary Domino Thinking* spell out P.E.P.P.R. *Put some spice into your life!*

CHAPTER 7

PRIMARY DOMINO THINKING
STEP 1

THE FIVE STEPS OF PRIMARY DOMINO THINKING

STEP 1: Passionate Possession

STEP 2: Exploration of the Problem or Issue

STEP 3: Producing the Primary Domino Thought

STEP 4: Primary Domino Thought Implantation

STEP 5: Regulation

PASSIONATE POSSESSION

To have impact, you must dare to get close.

In order to change something *you must first own it*. There is no other way. Many of us do not know how to actually take ownership because the natural initial response to any problem is to avoid it. Most of us have more practice in running away than in confronting. This chapter teaches you how to thoroughly and *passionately* possess a problem.

[Note: Whenever I use the word "problem" read that as *anything you prefer to change*.]

My neighbor across the street painted his house ochre. Ochre may qualify as my least favorite color. I have fantasies about going over there at 2:00 a.m. with a ladder, a brush, and five gallons of blue paint so that when I get up in the morning and face the day it's not an ochre day! But I don't "own" his house, so I cannot really do anything about his actual color choices. I can "own" my attitudes about ochre and change them, or I can make a decision to "own" the way I look out the windows and face a different way when I get up in the morning. I only have power over things I own.

A client was a raving alcoholic. His relationships with family members were a shambles, his finances were a disaster, his health was failing, and his work performance - on which he always had prided himself - was beginning to slip. His response to these difficulties was to a) blame others, bad luck, the weather, the government, and, b) drink more alcohol.

This client didn't think he had a drinking problem. In other words, he was in a state of *denial*. He could never personally do anything positive about these problems until he consciously began to "own" his situation. He had a long recovery road ahead of him and a casual approach was not about to effectively turn things around. He needed to *passionately possess* his alcoholism to see himself through the lean moments of recovery. This need for passionate possession is why some recovering alcoholics appear addicted to AA meetings for a few years; it is the very fervent attachment they need to sustain sobriety until they have internalized a new alcohol-free life.

In order to gain a foothold on a problem in your person or business, it must be possessed, and *the more significant the problem, the more passionate the possession must be.*

By not possessing a problem you "disempower yourself" which sounds a lot like "disemboweling yourself" doesn't it?

Any problem can be overcome if it can first be encircled and embraced. You can never solve your problems by distancing yourself from them. The faster you run, the faster they run. It is with "The buck stops here!" mentality that change effectively begins. Please learn this NOW, once and for all. Here's how.

Three ways to passionately possess a problem

You can passionately possess a problem utilizing any one of the three ways. Any of the three will work alone. Put all three together and the problem doesn't stand a chance!

Willingness (preferences/demands)

Change originates within the self because of *willingness*. Without willingness not much changes. This is because humans are made from molecules and are, therefore, somewhat subject to the laws of physics. The Law of Inertiain physics states: "That which is at rest remains at rest until some force operates upon it. Also, that which is in motion remains in motion until some force operates upon it." This means that we have a tendency to keep doing (or not-doing) the same things over and over, until we develop the willingness to change. We just maintain a routine until one type of willingness or another raises its head and provides the impetus for change. It behooves you to understand that there are different forms of willingness.

There are different types of willingness, each being a different mind-emotion state.

WILLINGNESS 1 - Seeking relief

The state of being in which we are at some level of physical/emotional/mental pain and are in need of specific relief. This is motivation based on either moving away from discomfort and/or towards the perceived source of remediation, e.g., water if we are thirsty, food if we are hungry, etc.

WILLINGNESS 2 - Need to achieve

We set a goal and are then "pulled" by it, e.g., getting a college degree, keeping a job, Saturday yard duties, personal 5-year plan, a business plan, etc.

WILLINGNESS 3 - Sensing realization of potential

An exploration into self-development involving higher levels of being, e.g., spiritual quests, vision quests, seeking of human potential experiences, etc.

Willingness 1 keeps you stuck.

Most adults are motivated by avoidance of painful consequences: "If I don't do _____, something bad will happen." Until they master and feel secure in their lower needs (food, water, warmth, companionship, etc.) people remain stuck with discomfort reduction, or Willingness 1, as a way of life. This is tragically ironic. The development of the ability to permanently master and control the supply of necessities becomes side-tracked by a constant preoccupation with just the "supply lines." People in this situation are generally so consumed with the necessity of obtaining relief from the demands of stress and insecurity that they often develop blinders to their potential as independently empowered entities.

One way to break this cycle is to base one's desires for change on *preferences* instead of on *demands*. It is significantly less stressful to say, "I *prefer* to do the dishes now." as opposed to "I *have* to do the dishes now." or "I *prefer* to have more money." rather than "I've *got to* have more money." This is because the second statement includes desperation and resentment. The first statement is imbued with the freedom to choose and have control over one's life.

It is preferable to upgrade your demands to preferences as it places you in an adult to adult relationship with yourself. This is better than a parent-child relationship with yourself based on "shoulds," "havetos," "musts," and "oughtas." These inner negative conversational patterns establish habits of alleviating discomfort with discomforting motivational systems, which will naturally create a need for more alleviation.

Preferences have to do with an individual's desire to change various aspects of his or her experience. There are many reasons a person may prefer self-designed change. These might include the need to:

a) be better equipped to achieve a goal

b) remove misery from one's life

c) repair damage from the past

d) feel better

e) have more fun

f) be creative

g) be challenged to actualize potentialities

h) increase one's effectiveness

i) lower distress levels

j) give a gift to oneself, another, or society.

It is much easier to launch change from a preferential state than from a demand state. You are encouraged to deliberately up-grade your willingness status from discomfort relief (Willingness 1) to a sense of empowered achievement (Willingness 2) or actualization of your potential (Willingness 3). This will lower emotional resistance, alleviate potential distress, and encourage self-responsibility.

Responsibility

One is obviously powerless to change things peacefully without being responsible for them in the first place. If I don't want to be on the Grounds Committee, then I forfeit my opportunity to decide where the new shrubbery will be placed. If I want to be able to do something about my anger, then it is in my best interest to *own* my anger. If I am uncomfortable with my child's behavior, it is smart to mentally acknowledge my part in co-creating the situation.

Responsibility is an *investment*. To take responsibility for everything that happens in your life is an investment in *you*. Taking responsibility doesn't mean we are unable to hold others accountable for their behaviors. It does mean we definitely hold ourselves accountable for what we do with our life here and now, i.e., if somebody drops a hot potato in your lap, your first "response-ability" should be to take care of yourself. If you lose a body part in an accident caused by another person's carelessness, it is in your best interests to concentrate on what you are going to do with you now, rather than concentrating on self-pity or repetitive fantasies of retaliation.

Intellectually, it makes sense to be responsible for everything that directly affects you; if you sit with the hot potato in your lap while blaming the culprit, you will have a different future than if you choose instead to make potato salad while waiting for your lawyer to return your call.

CLUE:
At any moment in time you are either responsible or you are a victim - it is your choice.

Most people don't like the word *responsibility* because as children we never heard it said with a smile. It was always toned as burdensome or laborious. Our poor ancestors carried around that false puritanical thinking, and even felt they were handing us a gift with the attitude: "Suffer big loads of responsibility and someday you will be rewarded." Maybe that half-truth worked well enough to keep them going, but not without a lot of wear and tear, as you have probably observed. The part of the half-truth that is true is that responsibility *is* good; the part of the half-truth that is not true is that responsibility should be a burden.

Another CLUE:
Responsibility is the key to liberation.

Again, you have no control over modifying that for which you are not responsible. Having no responsibility over a situation is akin to being a victim in that particular situation. This book is mostly concerned with your internal state from which all things flow (or don't flow) for you. When speaking of responsibility know that it begins *within*, even if the observable results of responsible behavior are seen *without*.

Responsibility begins with thought. So let's have a new thinking about responsibility. No matter who or what you have been blaming for your condition, your problems, your emotions, your whatever, up until now, rest assured that it is in your best interest to believe the following from now on:

"I love everything about being responsible for everything I experience or refrain from experiencing!"

It is important to memorize this and think it to yourself 20 times a day no matter how much you currently dispute it. After a few days (or only minutes if you are a fast learner), when you see the truth and power of this thought, you will have a wonderful experience of empowerment. You won't need to repeat it anymore because you will **know** it to be true.

If after a few days you still have trouble accepting it by just thinking about it, write it out ten times a day. When you "get it" you will smile or laugh.

This realization alone is worth a fortune. Without this realization, I assure you that very few vital wonderful things are going to happen by your design in life.

A special note:

This affirmative form of thinking about responsibility is not about inducing guilt, as does the belief, "I have cancer and I created it in myself." Affirmations, such as the one above, are used to induce empowerment, for example, "I now own this cancer and I can do something about it!" Once again, it is difficult, if not impossible, to do anything about something you don't own.

Also, when we discuss responsibility, we are NOT talking about:

- **revenge** - as some do when they attempt to decide who "the responsible party" was, or
- **resentment** - unresolved anger expressing itselfas when we say, "Aha, *you* are the one who was responsible," or
- **righteousness** - "It wasn't *my* fault!", or the flipside of righteousness,
- **regret** (guilt) - "Oh, [sob] it was *my* fault."

What we are discussing is, *Who is going to own your life?* It is a business-like decision: Are you or aren't you going to own, direct, produce and star in your own positive and productive drama called *your life*?

And another CLUE: Either you are responsible, or you are responsible for being irresponsible.

Now wouldn't you just know it? There is no escaping responsibility! Even if you have been victimized you are still responsible for what you are going to do with that incident.

And still yet another CLUE: All woundings are not self-inflicted, but all healings are.

Some victims are not aware that they help fertilize their own victimization through self-pity, self-inflicted reenactments, denial, the four R's (revenge, resentment, righteousness and regret), or unwillingness to pursue healing. *Primary Domino Thinking* facilitate your overcoming all these reasons for staying in misery.

Big CLUE: Responsibility is empowering, and the more you have, the more you'll have of what you want.

If you choose not to own something, you lose the right to change it. If you choose not to own something you either must run from it (not good), suppress it's effects on you (not good), continue to be victimized by it (not good) or *detach* from it (good). Later, the second step of *Primary Domino Thinking* will show you how to detach.

Conscious Connected Breathing (CCB)

If you are unwilling to possess the problem, and you feel unable to assume responsibility for the problem, and are, as a result, still blocked from possessing the problem, there is one surefire methodfor taking ownership.

VERY IMPORTANT NOTE: Breathing is central to life and Conscious Connected Breathing is central to the efficacy of *Primary Domino Thinking*. Learn the following well by using it often. It has many, many benefits.

Do the following:

Keep your breathing circular
...no pauses between the inhale and exhale...
*As you read this take in a slow full breath
...a little more...
...and a little more still...
Gently and slowly, that's it...
Now, after your chest is fairly full...
Let go of your breath so that your chest slowly goes down...
Refrain from controlling the exhale in any way...
...just let the exhale come out by itself...
When your chest is almost empty
go back to the * in the   italicized part of this
paragraph and do it again nine more times.
(Yes, nine more times.)

Notice how you feel differently after doing this just ten times. Whatever you are feeling you are feeling *different*, aren't you? Just ten consciously connected breaths with a relaxed exhale, provides a noticeable shift. That differencecan also be called *acceptance*, because this is the way you breathe when you are in a happy/serene/peaceful frame of mind, i.e., "accepting what is so." The reason CCB is so powerful is that it allows you to accept situations your mind usually rejects, thus overcoming *one* major roadblock in terms of influencing that situation.

Note that "accepting" something is not the same as "affirming" it: *Acceptance* encircles something so that you can change it if you prefer, and *affirmation* means that you like something just the way it is. For example, I can accept that you smoke cigarettes (I know you must really *need* them or you wouldn't be doing this to yourself!), although I prefer you to change. If I *affirm* your smoking, I believe it's a great idea for you to do this to yourself!

Again, the advantage of accepting something you would normally reject gives you control over how it is going to influence you. If you reject anything, you have no choice but to run from it until you are forced to accept it or until you fall into a grave.

Although it is so familiar to you, breathing is very different from other body functions. It is a body function that happens automatically *or* it can be done with deliberate consciousness. Heartbeats, digestion, circulatory functions, body temperature regulation, neural transmissions, etc., are difficult to take over and perform consciously. Breathing, on the other hand, can be taken over in the blink of an eye and, in this case, used to your definite advantage: the advantage of always being at *choice* rather than being at *no-choice*.

CLUE:

In order to effectively and deliberately redesign your world, you must always come from a position of choice.

One of the primary signs of life is whether you are breathing or not. Breath is more significant in your life than the other three forms of required life force energy: water, sunlight or food. If you need proof, ask yourself this question: "Of breath, water, sunlight or food, which am I willing to go an hour without?"

Breathing has another significant function; it is a barometer monitored by your brain in an ongoing evaluation of your current life situation. When you feel threatened you hold your breath or breathe shallowly. Notice the way you breathe the next time you balance your checkbook! On the other hand, when we feel at peace, as when watching a beautiful sunset or experiencing "afterglow," we breathe fully and slowly.

Because you can make a conscious choice to change your breathing pattern to benefit you, and since the autonomic nervous system reads your body language (especially your mode of breathing) to see if there is cause for alarm (and need for subsequent fight or flight tension), *it is in your best interests to breathe slowly and fully as often as you can remember to do so.*

Slow and full breathing sends a physiological message of serenity to your muscles, circulatory system and glands, even if you are in a stressful situation. Most of us have grown up succumbing to a natural reaction of contracting our breathing again and again in response to fearful conditions and, upon reaching adulthood, have developed a habit pattern of shallow broken breathing which sends a constant message of panic to the blind autonomic nervous system.

Conscious connected breathing restores your physical-emotional-mental state to that of a baby-at-peace - like you once were - *while empowering you at the same time.* This last statement will certainly challenge any of you who are still carrying around the notion that being perpetually tense and hypervigilant keeps you in control and safe. It doesn't (don't you have enough proof by now?) because being tense and hypervigilant is a *victim stance,* and invites perpetrators like a blood in the water attracts sharks.

Let me assure you that you are very well-equipped to respond to an emergency from a relaxed CCB state. A cat - even one who never works out - can change from a totally limp posture into an instant lightning bolt of action at the mere hint of a mouse sighting. You, too, can go from a relaxed state to instant action, if needed, without being on guard all the time.

Conscious Connected Breathing (CCB) Guidelines

1) Connect the inhale and exhale "at both ends," keeping the breathing totally circular. Sometimes it helps to have a visual image inside your

head. Some people use a thought-picture of a connected white string continuously circling. One person thought of bicycle pedals going round and round.

2) Relax the exhale, refraining from controlling the exhale with the stomach, chest, throat or lips. *Just let the air exit of its own accord.* Surprisingly, this may take concentrated practice. Discovering just how much you have been conditioned over the years to eke out your exhale can be a real eye-opener. Practice until the exhale is naturally easy and free.

Do this:
Stack up your vertebrae and close your eyes (after you read this) and breathe fully and connectedly for five minutes.

Notice after about thirty seconds (when you begin to feel good) how your mind wants you to get busy with something else. This is an excellent example of how reflexively we like to rain on our own parade!

3) If you experience uncomfortable dizziness the first few times you do CCB, don't take in quite so much air. If you like being dizzy, then breathe deeper. Dizziness disappears after the first few times of doing CCB.

4) Do CCB whenever you think of it. Good times to practice are while waiting in line or at a railroad crossing. Utilize CCB during times of tension when you feel out of control, such as when getting a speeding ticket, interviewing for a new job, facing your boss, arguing with your (or anybody else's) spouse, or worrying about anything in the universe.

5) CCB is a terrific way to control insomnia. By merely relaxing and doing slow-and-full conscious connected breathing, you will drift off to sleep or, at the very least, you will feel so peaceful you won't care if you remain awake.

6) CCB is a great way to start your day. Arise five minutes earlier than usual, sit on the floor or in a chair with your back straight, and do 5 minutes of conscious connected breathing. Notice the difference in your morning!

7) Slow and full breathing is the most peaceful. If you are filled with fear or anger and cannot seem to hold a lot of air, still keep your breathing connected until you can breathe more deeply; then do so for at least five minutes to help resolve residual emotions from the previous episode.

8) Practicing and playing with CCB over time will prove to you what a natural power source you possess 24 hours a day. It can become your

way of being a constantly nurturing and empowering companion to yourself.

Step 1 Summary

Step 1 gives three methods for owning a problem. When you determine that something needs changing *that* is a problem. Life is full of problems. Life may even *be* problems. One thing is certain: You are unable to do anything about a problem if you don't know how to make it part of your reality by getting close to it.

SUMMARY CLUE:

The more positively and passionately you accept a problem as part of your reality, the more power you possess for changing it.

The degree to which one is effective at problem-solving is not only related to acceptance, but also to the enthusiasm of that acceptance. Basically, enthusiasm is willingness, responsibility and Conscious Connected Breathing on a rheostat. The more you turn these three up at any moment, the more enthused you will feel about possessing the problem in that moment and the more effective you will be in solving the problem, too.

Yet another CLUE:

Your only choice at any one moment is to passionately possess what is happening in the NOW, or to procrastinate doing so - it is always up to you, and only you.

This and the next four chapters each cover a phase of *Primary Domino Thinking*. To facilitate absorption of this powerful vehicle for change, an ongoing Step example from real life (name changed) will be given at the end of each of these chapters to illustrate the progressive utilization of *Primary Domino Thinking*.

Please select a problem of your own that you have not yet resolved and experiment along as your own case study. Write in your name and then journal through each of the five steps as each chapter ends.

Step 1 Example:

Adam finally reached 50 years of age, but not without some scars and burdens. Although successful, the price tag has left its marks. Adam still does not feel good about himself even if, by most standards, he should: two kids raised, two advanced degrees, two cars (paid for), a nice home (half paid for), a wonderful wife and a highly respected profession and standing in the community. After all the smoke has cleared from his strivings, he now has time to reflect upon his feelings of incompletion. At first, he blames his office staff's occasional incompetence or his wife's mood swings or his golf score, but more and more he feels the finger pointing at himself.

Doing an extended session with Conscious Connected Breathing Adam begins to feels tears forming in his eyes and realizes that something inside is obviously out of harmony. It is at this moment that he knows that he must take ownership of his issues if he is to resolve this feeling of incompletion.

YOUR STORY:

You: Select an issue in your life that has been unresolved despite your best efforts so far, and fill out the journal spaces below. At the end of the next four chapters there will be room for you to continue developing your *Primary Domino Thinking* solution. Watch how your issue finally gets resolved!

A) Describe the problem to be possessed:

_____

_____

_____

_____

B) Describe your level of willingness: (See page 56.)

_____

_____

_____

_____

C) Begin Conscious Connected Breathing, reflect on your problem and continue doing so for 5 minutes - no less.

D) Reflect on what you have written in A & B and modify them if necessary.

_____

_____

_____

_____

E) Do more CCB and say to yourself, "I own this problem - it is mine, all mine."

F) Allow yourself to own the problem physically and emotionally as well as mentally.

G) Why not officially begin your journal describing your ongoing experiences with *Primary Domino Thinking*. Include input from your five minute CCB session, and especially document your mental "grapplings" as you come to grips with your issue. This will be very helpful personal reference material for you later on. (It is always best to keep your journal entries confidential.)

CHAPTER 8

PRIMARY DOMINO THINKING
STEP 2

THE FIVE STEPS OF PRIMARY DOMINO THINKING

STEP 1: Passionate Possession

STEP 2: Exploration of the Problem or Issue

STEP 3: Producing the Primary Domino Thought

STEP 4: Primary Domino Thought Implantation

STEP 5: Regulation

EXPLORATION OF THE PROBLEM OR ISSUE

Investigate the problem, discovering who truly owns it.

Problems that are correctly assessed do not remain problems for very long. If a problem hangs around for awhile, it's a good bet that it has been inaccurately assessed. As a psychotherapist I have listened to, observed, and learned a great deal about problems.

Five Dynamics of Problems

1) If a client "knew" on our first meeting what the problem was, then more than likely that was *not* the problem! So, for now, figure that whatever issues have been bothering you for some time have probably been misdiagnosed.

This is usually true because a correctly stated problem has a built-in solution and people, being fairly smart, will immediately take steps to solve the problem, e.g., "I'm hungry because it has been five hours since I have eaten food. Solution: Eat some food." For many clients, once the problem was clarified our work together was finished, and they went off confidently to do what they knew clearly had to be done.

2) People often identify problems correctly but misidentify the true owner of the problem, e.g., "It drives me nuts when your room is a mess...what's wrong with you!" It does make you feel and even appear less than sane when you are trying to own and solve somebody else's problem...and this is a **very common** dilemma.

A client of mine had a female friend with compulsive behaviors that he kept trying to fix by pointing out her problems, giving her articles to read, arguing with her, manipulating situations, and even speaking with professionals on her behalf. Her compulsions worsened, so his response was to redouble his efforts. This strategy created even more compulsive energy until the woman was eventually spending over 8 hours a day in her behavior. He identified "his problem" as her behavior, which left him no recourse but to continue his unsuccessful efforts at controlling her. Against both their desires, the relationship, due to overwhelming frustration, wound up as an abusive one.

At issue was: To whom does the problem behavior belong? The answer was apparent: her behavior was her issue and hers alone. His problem was ignorance in knowing how to productively associate with a loved one burdened by compulsive behaviors. Once this realization became internalized by each of them, they were free to concentrate their energies on solutions that would really work.

3) Life provides an abundance of challenges called *problems*.

The quest in life is not to run out of problems, but to replace nit-picky problems with big juicy ones that let you know you are getting somewhere when you solve them! To constantly worry over the same rent payment every month is a nit-picky problem that is endless, with only a temporary reprieve at best. Every time you "solve" this problem by finally paying the rent, your mind knows that the problem truly has not gone away, but is just hibernating for a few weeks. A nice juicy problem is to raise your level of income by getting a college education or embarking on a new job search; this produces a sense of "mission-growth" which feels much more productive even if it does include shifting some new gears.

4) All problems can be solved if you are willing to: a) assess them accurately (including discovering ownership); b) chunk down the solution into right-size pieces; and c) be persistent in applying solutions.

This includes attempts at changing life situations or personal characteristics.

5) The major internal blocks to solving problems boil down to just two: *ignorance* and *stubbornness*. Either a person doesn't have enough knowledge about the problem and/or its solution (ignorance), or when the needed knowledge is obtained, the person is unyielding in their old patterns and refuses to apply what could work (stubbornness). Many humans are more concerned with being *right* about notchanging destructive patterns than being healthy and happy. Strange as it may seem, people often choose to die rather than change.

Here lies
Willie Smith.
Dead of Terminal
Righteousness.
He has lots of company.

Step 2-A

Problem Identification: Assessing the situation

The assessment phase is where precision begins to play a critical role in the deliberate self-design process. If the key area of concern cannot be accurately pinpointed, you are left with an ineffective strategy akin to shooting at noises in the dark, or, worse still, shooting at the wrong target in the light. These strategies of random-shooting and wrong-targeting are, of course, the most often used approaches to problem-solving. This explains why many problems are never satisfactorily solved. One can only begin to wonder if there isn't a hidden investment in *non-solution* in these cases. Parents who continually find things to criticize in their children may have a need to have power over something they can control, so it really doesn't matter how much the kids improve. There will be no end to the criticism. The *source* of the tirades may be the real problem and not the child's spotlighted behavior.

CLUE:

You never discover the source of light by following the beam to where it is pointing.

A graduate program at a small college in Ohio could not understand why they didn't get their fair share of the college's marketing budget. Month after month they blamed themselves for not presenting a good case to administration, or they blamed the publicity director (the college president's right-hand man) for being prejudiced against the graduate division. As their enrollment began to dwindle, they also blamed other colleges for cutting into their territory. Crazy feelings and criticism abounded until three years later it was uncovered that the college president had a secret clause in his contract that he received a yearly bonus which was based, not on total enrollment figures, but on undergraduate enrollment *only*. Suddenly the problem was clear. It was now obvious why the graduate program was not mentioned in general college advertising and publicity releases and received so little coverage in campus newspapers and magazines mailed out to the public. Once the problem was correctly assessed, the graduate division began altering their attack on the problem by convincing the president that the graduate program's success would increase the attractiveness of the school to potential undergraduate enrollees. Almost miraculously, many of the graduate program's marketing concerns began moving toward resolution.

Back in Step 1 you assumed possession of a problem passionately in order to get close enough to determine *true ownership* of the problem. Upon further investigation in Step 2 it may be discovered that you actually do *not* own the problem formerly possessed in Step 1. If this is found to be true, a solution known as "giving it back" could now be instituted.

Giving it back is a proactive mindset that liberates you to get on with important things and provides a great deal of mental relief. It is the security of, once and for all, knowing that an issue is truly no longer your problem. This allows you to lift the burden from your shoulders and to walk away free of the necessity of finding a solution. In addition to mentally giving it back, you can also formally and verbally give it back. This means engaging a person in person, over the telephone, or via mail, and informing them that: "This issue about _____ is not MY problem - it could be YOURS." Use these words pretty much verbatim.

If they do not accept the problem, that is not your problem either. But if you have to live or work with that person, then you may experience Fred's challenge of learning to live with someone who has a problem and doesn't take care of it. If you let their ineptitude at problem ownership bother you, then THIS becomes your problem. But this is much, much easier to handle than attempting to solve the problem that wasn't yours in the first place!

> *"Attempting to solve someone else's problem is as futile as trying to convince your mother that you are, indeed, now grown up."*
> -Anon

Three Blocks to Accurate Assessment

It is so important to get off on the right foot in diagnosing a problem, that it is in your best interests to closely examine some reasons for potential difficulty in doing so. As you read along, think of real examples from your own experiences which exemplify these blocks.

1) Dishonesty as a Block to Accurate Assessment

Integrity is rare. Lack of *integrity* (inaccurate or incomplete disclosure) exists because of fear-filled childhood experiences of being punished for being honest. Fear of disclosure is based upon a belief that "If the truth be known, I will suffer pain in some form." By the time humans have reached adulthood they have seen ample proof of this, and have evolved elaborate schemes to fool others and themselves.

It is unfortunate that children often get punished for just being themselves. All child abuse and neglect is received by children as a message that "You are not good enough the way you are." A child's fear and/or willingness to please is their first sacrifice of integrity: "I shall pretend to *be* (think/feel/do) someone I am not." Children are reinforced in this strategy by the subsequent withdrawal of the punishment or even by being rewarded with a smile, a goody, or a loving touch, thus imbedding the strategy of *sacrificing integrity for the sake of relieving pain or gaining reward.* It worked then - it may have even been seen as the only way to stay alive - and it still works for adults treating each other and themselves like children. But nothing works as well as honesty.

CLUE:
Now that you are an adult you can lay aside childhood strategies for surviving and being loved, and you will be safe.

Oh, you may get a few raised eyebrows because you suddenly get honest, since people will probably notice a definite change in you. But I haven't heard of anyone being killed by a raised eyebrow since back in '06!

We must exhibit here in Step 2 the same willingness that we utilized in Step 1 to passionately possess the problem in order to answer the question: "Honestly, just what is the real problem here?" Refuse to accept your own snappy answers. If you instantly feel you have the answer to an ongoing problem, that's probably *not* the answer. Be willing to get even more honest - and more honest still.

2) Avoidance as a Block to Accurate Assessment

The usual human strategy for dealing with a problem is best described as "running like hell." Unfortunately problems have a way of running as fast as your shadow, so this strategy has largely proven ineffective. Reliable identification mandates a willingness to *focus* on the problem...to be *with* the problem...to *get close* enough to the problem to notice how it ticks. This means rejecting avoidance strategies such as ignoring, daydreaming, fantasizing, changing the subject, quick judgment dispensation, "ozoning," medicating with the ingestion of food/alcohol/nicotine/drugs/etc., "problem-hopping," or compulsive habits.

> *Oh no! If you are going to take all those customary and comfortable patterns of avoidance away, what's left?*

Instead, sit quietly with an assessment mentality while doing Conscious Connected Breathing and you will eventually know what you need to know. Have faith in the ability of this simple strategy. It is easy and effective.

CLUE:

Peel the onion to the core and there will be no more tears or fears.

3) Insufficient Information as a Block to Accurate Assessment

You are limited (*limit* = how far you let yourself go) to the amount of information you have available to you at any one moment. Herein lies the intrinsic worth of true education: It gives an individual more choices.

Choice is where the power is.

Ignorance in a particular situation means a lack of internal tools and skills (information and processes) to modify that situation. It is in your best interests to have enough *humility* (knowing your current limits) and willingness to continually expand your knowledge base. "Problems" present the opportunity and motivation to do just this (providing a good enough reason to be grateful for the next problem that you are fortunate enough to have come your way!).

Each problem solved expands your holdings and your chances for success in the next problem arena, and so on and so on, exponentially.

In other words, sometimes it behooves you to *learn*, in the classic sense, about a problem by reading, asking, pondering, researching, digging, and absorbing. Not to worry: If you don't have the necessary motivation to seek out new information, Step 4 will often create that drive in you, sometimes seemingly out of nowhere.

A practice session with assessment

In this practice session you are going to play with assessment. Eventually you will be adept at doing this quickly, but for now just absorb it one step at a time. For this exercise we will define "problem" as *anything which one is challenged to change.* As an example, if I notice I am thirsty, that is not a problem although it is a situation calling for change. If I am thirsty and I am unable to find water, *that* is a problem because it is a potentially difficult challenge. Decisions are not problems - unless you have a problem making decisions.

DO THIS: Sit straight up in a quiet place and do one minute of CCB. Relax your body and your thinking...just let everything *be*. After one minute or so, when you feel open to exploration, spend a little time selecting a problem in your personal life that you would like to change (not the same one you are using at the end of the Step chapters). Clearly focus on the problem and make it real as you can in your mind. This is called *bringing definition to the problem.*

Now as you breathe connectedly with a relaxed exhale ask yourself this question:

"Who really owns this problem?" [ALWAYS contemplate for at least 10 seconds prior to answering!]

If the answer is someone other than yourself go to i) below.

If the answer is, *"I own this problem."* go to ii) below.

i) Continuing the process along with the CCB and relaxation, ask yourself: *"What does taking on another's problem have to offer me?"*

Be ruthless in listening for all the answers you will hear - there can be many so hear them all. Some will be weird, some will seem silly, some will not please you, but the objective here is to provide an audience for *all* of them.

If after you listen to the answers you decide that you have no interest in continuing possessing other people's problems in futility, decide how you are going to "give back" the problem (which was never yours in the first place!). Then make a *commitment* to do that, with a definitive time at which it will be done.

If you are still unable to let go of someone's problem, then *your* problem can be defined as "meddling" in other people's problems - you may go on to ii and you can use *that* as your problem. [End of i]

ii) Continue the process along with CCB and relaxation.

Now ask yourself:

"What do I gain by having this problem?"

Be willing to hear all the answers no matter how unusual they may be, and be willing to own them all no matter how they make you feel. This is called *ownership of the problem*. This gets you ready for Step 3 in the next chapter. [End of ii]

Realize that in order to be effective with *Primary Domino Thinking*, you need flexibility and a general refraining from "hair-trigger assessments" involving snappy ego-driven explanations and solutions. The need to be right is inherent in all of us, and that is not only good, but necessary, for survival. But when we are stubbornly insistent on "being right," we will soon fall victim to our own ego and it will be, without a doubt, painful and confusing. Have enough humility from the beginning to suspend judgment until you have taken in the whole scene. You have everything to gain by having patience.

Step 2-B

Problem Identification: Expanding the number of possible explanations

It is interestingly tragic how people can be so snappy with solutions that do not work and how slow they can be to realize this. Sadly, many proposed "solutions" are actually just poor attempts at explanation. These explanations become futile attempts to solve a dilemma.

For example,

a) "I don't feel good about my finances but I just can't stop spending."

b) "I can't find peace - my neighbors drive me crazy."

c) "My interest in spirituality is lagging - churches are filled with only pseudo-Christians these days."

Notice how externally located the implied solutions are in these explanations.

a) Spending controls how I feel.

b) The neighbors are in charge of how peaceful I can feel.

c) Others are in charge of my spiritual development.

If you locate potential cures for your problems "out there," the results are usually zero. Problems are usually not "out there" and, if they were, the solution would be probably be obvious.

BIG CLUE: *Problems are located within.*

Believing anything other than this is a disowning of the problem. Disowning the problem leaves one powerless to do anything reasonable and workable about it. It is no wonder people acting to solve their problems on the basis of constant misdiagnosis begin to feel, and even appear, nutty. For a good graphic representation of this, imagine what would happen if you dropped a brick on your foot but for some reason located the pain in your right ear. There you are hobbling around looking for ear treatment, trying to convince everyone (and yourself) that there really *is* a problem with your ear. Can you relate this to anything in your life?

You say, "But some problems really are 'out there.' If a car breaks down, **it** is causing me a problem and I get angry." Your statement is that *car breakdowns upset me*, which is simply not true. The next time you are driving somewhere and you see someone at the side of the road with a stalled car, notice that you are probably not upset!

"Upsets" are emotions which arise from challenging circumstances. They are created by two things: a) a violation of our expectations; and/or b) a remembrance of unfinished business from our past. Interestingly enough, we own both our expectations and our unfinished business! In other words, *you*cannot upset me, only *I* can upset me because of my expectations (which I can control, if I so choose), or by my history (which is all mine and can be healed, if I so choose - see *Resolving Unfinished Business* in Bibliography). It is an incredibly liberating thought to know that you (and only you) can control all of your upsets. *A special note on boundaries*

Humans are supposed to develop a concept of *boundary*, an immediate territory around themselves that they reside in, maintain, and control. At birth we didn't have a good sense of boundary as we couldn't take care of ourselves. We had to rely on others who were supposed to maintain and control us *for a while* until we took control of ourselves. Since everyone around us was bigger, more experienced and more powerful, we let them have their way. Our other choice was to die.

Nurturing and intelligent caregivers facilitate their children's development of a sense of independence and healthy self-maintenance as they grow older. As adults, children raised in this manner are capable of not only running their lives successfully but also raising their eventual offspring so that they can run their own lives as well. This implies that a healthy child gradually develops a set of internal tools and external skills in order to operate with stability inside their boundaries and to interact meaningfully outside of them.

Unfortunately, for many of us this was not the case. Even from the best of homes we were conditioned codependently to trust others or things - luck, fate, nature, deities - more than ourselves, and we never fully actualized our true *independence* - our natural birthright. We learned enough to get by, and get by we do, but *just getting by is not our destiny.*

CLUE: *Those who live to just get by never realize their destiny to fly.*

Understandably many humans have chosen to just get by *and that is their right.* We always have the choice of living below our potential. Another choice is to move in the direction of realizing our potential. If we choose the latter, it mandates that we locate the source of our problems inside ourselves.

With all this in mind, let us return to our quest for *expanding the realm of possible explanations* within our own system of thinking.

Unless you quickly and accurately assesses the root cause of a problem (in which case you can usually skip Step 2 and go right to Step 3) it is essential to suspend judgment long enough to do some reflective thinking, which is what the old "Count to 10" adage was all about. Know that the first step in contemplation is *restraint* - refraining from reaching a "quick and dirty" answer until all the possibilities are in. But, if after 'restraining' for a while, no explanation yet makes sense, then more drastic measures are necessary! Get out a pencil and a piece of paper.

The Listing Method

Write the problem at the top of a sheet of paper. State it as clearly and specifically as you can. Then, while performing Conscious Connected Breathing, write 20 reasons, *as quickly as you can*, why this problem might exist. Don't think or hesitate, just write *anything,* no matter how crazy or funny it may sound to you. This process gets you past those mental blocks that keep you from the truth.

Example:

Problem: I can't stop eating pastry.

1) I love it!

2) It makes me feel good.

3) I deserve it.

4) I was never allowed to eat it when I was a child.

5) It prevents boredom.

6) It gives me energy.

7) It helps me to forget things because it keeps me busy.

8) It keeps me from being successful in my desire to be trim.

9) I get to shop for it.

10) It's a way of rewarding myself.

11) Nobody can tell me when and how much I get to eat it.

12) It curbs my appetite.

13) It gives me another excuse to hate myself.

14) It's MINE, all MINE (I don't have to share it with anybody).

15) It brings out the little kid in me.

16) It brings back fond memories.

17) I just have a sweet tooth.

18) It's my private stroke to myself.

19) I'm addicted to it.

20) Rebellion: It proves that I can eat anything I want!

Step 2-C

Problem Identification: Select the most accurate of the explanations

Perhaps there was an "aha!" experience even while you were doing The Listing Method. If so, then this would move you into Step 3 of *Primary Domino Thinking*. If you did not have the "aha," then do the listing again with different answers and this time really push it outlandishly (and don't forget to breathe).

If this second attempt didn't provide the "aha!" look over what you have written so far and, while CCBing, select the one that is most meaningful to you. You are now ready for Step 3.

Step 2 - Example:

Remember Adam, the successful business man with everything going for him - except he feels badly inside? Adam has now given up on the Blaming Method as a way of solving his discontent. Being intelligent he has noticed that no matter how much he blames, things do not get better - often they actually get worse. Utilizing the Listing Method, Adam runs through the exercise twice and notices a pattern. He is actually depressed! He is led to do some reading on men's depression in their middle years.

YOUR STORY:

Do the practice session with assessment on page 89.

Perform the listing method (page 95) on your problem.

Select the most accurate explanation of your chosen problem from the listing method and write it here:

_____

_____

_____

_____

Summary

Problems are "hot." People want to dump them as fast as they arrive despite all the cliches such as "Life is problems," "We grow through problems," You learn from your mistakes," "Problems build character," etc. Most of us have a hard time sitting with a problem long enough to let it fully develop, not unlike a photograph in the developer, gradually coming clearly into focus. Men, in particular, are raised to be competitively project and problem-solver oriented as one of their main ego-strengths. There's nothing wrong with this, but sometimes these traits rush the process towards solution too rapidly to allow the true problem to emerge.

Whoever said *"Patience is a virtue"* must have been talking about problem-solving, because it is certainly good and pertinent advice. Sitting quietly for five minutes and reflecting on a problem, or consciously putting a problem onto your "backburner" and sleeping on it, can often produce astounding results.

CHAPTER 9

PRIMARY DOMINO THINKING
STEP 3

THE FIVE STEPS OF *PRIMARY DOMINO THINKING*

STEP 1: Passionate Possession

STEP 2: Exploration of the Problem or Issue

STEP 3: Producing the Primary Domino Thought

STEP 4: Primary Domino Thought Implantation

STEP 5: Regulation

PRODUCING THE PRIMARY DOMINO

"Generate your magic formula."

If there is a consistent formula for having the life you want it must always first include *ownership* and *clarification* of the obstructions, or problems, that are getting in the way. The previous chapters were dedicated to clearing away the fog around these two important criteria for success. Step 1 of *Primary Domino Thinking* is about the how-to of passionate possession. Step 2 shows you how to get a grip on the exact identity of the problem.

If it has been determined that the problem is not "mine," then the problem has, by now, been surrendered to the proper authorities. But if the problem has found its home in you, and you have gained some decent clarity on its makeup then you are ready for Step 3.

Formulation

Step 3 is also known as the *formulation phase*. Don't let that scare you with its technological ring. It just means that in Step 3 you are going to design a shorter version of the problem explanation you derived in Step 2. We call this shorter version the *modifier* and the process of creating that modifier iscalled *formulation* because we are beginning to form the magical agent of automatic change in your life - the *actual Primary Domino Thought*.

The *modifier* is very important. It is, in effect, the beginning agent of change in *Primary Domino Thinking*. Considering the *modifier's* importance, obviously the process of developing it deserves special attention.

Are you starting to feel like a scientist? In effect, you *are* becoming a scientist - experimenting with yourself (which is what a lot of scientists actually do). Enter into it with that spirit, and see what you will discover in this wonderful laboratory: *Yourself.*

At this point I want to offer some notes of encouragement:

I understand that this procedure may look a little tedious, but it won't be for long. Once you internalize this, it will go more quickly every time you utilize it. And you will carry the tools to transform your life with you from now on!

I understand we all look for short fast answers that promise immediate and permanent relief. But be honest: How many fulfill the promise? None.

With *Primary Domino Thinking* you are altering your life permanently into a whole new healthy way of being. It takes a little learning, time, and patience, but I assure you *this is as easy as it gets*, and the dedication is really not much compared to the rewards that will open to you if you just stick with it.

Give yourself permission to materialize what you need in order to have what you really want and deserve.

We will take it step-by-step. Just follow along. You are about to learn some of the inner workings of human consciousness and how it can deliberately create your *reality*. It is simple, but exact. Pay close attention.

This may feel like we are turning around the world here, putting you at cause rather than effect in ways you never consciously dreamed of before. It's obviously going to create some mind-torque to bring this transformative state about, so be willing to commit to both the adventure and the work it takes if you want the benefits.

A Common Story

Imagine that you want to construct a building as your end product. You have hired workers and meet them the first day at the construction site at 7:00 a.m. You say to them, "Build me a building on this lot someday," and then you leave giving no further instructions. What kind of product will you get?

Let's take it further. You come back every week and notice the dismal results, and rant and rave about the "poor help these days," how "nothing works in my life," and "you better do what I want or else!" and then leave again without listening to the workers' feedback. As the days go by, you feel more and more frustrated, more disappointed, and maybe even more fatigued about your project. Despite all this energy going into the project, you sadly note that it still isn't coming about like you wanted it to. You finally surrender to a sense of depression, and just scrap the whole affair.

You nurse your wounds and save up your energy for a while, and then once again remind yourself that you should get going with something worthwhile in your life. You decide to start a new project.

You buy another lot, hire some new workers, meet them on-site at 7:00 a.m. and say, "Build me a building on this lot someday," and then you leave giving no further instructions. Sound familiar?

The mind makes a great slave, but not always so great a master, so in Step 3 we put the mind to work as the laborer for which it was intended. In other words, how can we make the mind effective at carrying out our plans?

One of brain's passengers is a little engine, best known as a "mind." The mind has many capabilities, but those capabilities are best served by a certain type of very specific instruction. If you say to the mind, "I want to be slim/wealthy/healthy/smart etc.," and walk away and expect the mind to do something with that vagueness, then you have some learning to do. *Primary Domino Thinking* is a very specific way of getting maximum performance from your mind-engine. Learn it well, and the mind will deliver unto you what you want, as a good paid employee should.

Step 3-A
Converting the explanation of your problem into a *modifier*

A simple but essential conversion is called for once the most accurate explanation for a particular problem has been arrived at in Step 2 above. The conversion is similar to the preparation of food for assimilation into the body - a process we call *digestion*, a series of food transformations starting with chewing and swallowing. The conversion from a Step 2 explanation of the problem to the development of a Step 3 *modifier* is known as *formulation*.

This consists of rephrasing the explanation into a *proactive positive solution* statement. If, for example, you selected "It curbs my appetite" as the reason for overindulging in sweets, then a potential *modifier* might be "I am as full as I healthfully need to be."

To further get the flavor of this, some examples will help clarify this part of Step 3. The *modifier* in each example listed below is italicized beneath each problem statement. *It is the exact opposite of the problem!*

Problem statement:

I get angry when ignored because I feel unimportant.

Modifier: *I am always important.*

Problem statement:

I don't feel good because I am overweight.

Modifier: *I have a sleek physique.*

Problem statement:

I hate this work because my job is boring.

Modifier: *This work excites me.*

Problem statement:

I am uncomfortable because my lower back is tense.

Modifier: *My back is relaxed and loose.*

Problem statement:

Thoughts of mother irritate me. She is always critical.

Modifier: *My mother cares about me.*

Yes, you are correct, your initial gut-level reaction to a *modifier* might be 'Ridiculous!' or 'B.S.!' or 'How stupid!'.

Let me assure you that most modifiers will only be so distained by you for a short while - until they come true!

To test a potential *modifier*, ask yourself, "Would the problem disappear if one could actually make the modifier come true?" If it would, then you know you have arrived at an appropriate *modifier*. If not, then restructure the *modifier* so that it does.

Understand that **the whole purpose of *Primary Domino Thinking* is to make the *modifier* become absolutely true in your life.**

So, it is important to take the time necessary to arrive at a good, solid *modifier* that is exactly the opposite of the problem.

Guidelines for Great Modifiers

We usually try to make changes in our life by using the inefficient trial and error method. Because of this inefficiency of trial and error methodology there is a reasonable guarantee of large amounts of wearing and tearing, not to mention terribly poor odds of success.

Most people just give up and "settle for" what they already have. This is why there is so little change in people's lives despite their pain, and how most of us become so adept at just "living with it" as our major form of expertise in life adjustment skills.

It is very, very smart to narrow the number of error trials as much as possible by utilizing your intelligence to select and sharpen the most appropriate *modifier*.

Modifiers are *affirmations*, a positive mirror image of the problem statement. There are different types and qualities of affirmations, and some can be very powerful just by themselves. Affirmations are positive thoughts which can be written, read and/or spoken. The purpose of an affirmation is to replace a negative, self abusive, stress-producing, disempowering thought with a positive, self-enhancing, empowering one. Since all behavior begins with thoughts it appears to be a good investment to make sure the roots of behavior are healthy and enjoyable. How do you determine if your *modifier* is a good one? Here are eight guidelines to help you test your *modifiers*.

1) **Personal:** You can only modify yourself. Do not try to affirm qualities or changes in other people to correct or alter situations you cannot control. In developing *modifiers*, you are changing your creative *modus operandi* through personal positive statements. In most cases a *modifier* should be an "I" statement.

2) **Positive:** Use only positive language in your *modifier*. It helps to write it out so you can see the words. Do not describe what you are trying to move away from or eliminate. Do not use words like *not, never, none,* etc.

3) **Present tense:** *Modifiers* should be stated in the present tense. The reason present tense must be used is that we are restructuring the subconscious mind and the present moment is the only time frame in which the subconscious operates. Avoid using future tense phrases such as "I will..." or "Someday..." "I'm going to..."

4) **Indicate achievement:** Do not indicate the ability, "I can," in your *modifier*, because this will not produce change. You already have the ability. What you must indicate concretely is actual achievement. Begin statements with "I am..." and "I have..."

5) **Action words:** Describe the activity you are modifying in terms that create pictures of you performing in an easy and anxiety free manner. Your subconscious actions should be described by statements that start with: "I easily," "I quickly," "I enjoy," "I love to," "I thrive on," and "I show" etc.

6) **Emotion words:** Try to put as much excitement in the wording of your *modifiers* as you can by vividly stating your behavior in colorful terms. Words that spark an emotional picture in your subconscious help

to make the experience in your *modifier* more believable, attractive and physical.

7) **Accuracy:** It is important for you to modify only as high as you can honestly imagine yourself becoming or performing. The rule of thumb is to not overshoot (too unrealistic to believe) or undershoot (sell yourself short). Just hold a clear and vivid picture of the end result you want to accomplish. Being accurate does not mean being perfectionistic. Your investment is not in perfection, but in excellence.

8) **Privacy:** Your modifications are personal and should be for yourself only. Others may constantly try to remind you of your old ways without really meaning to hold you back. Part of the power of *Primary Domino Thinking* is that people around you may get "upset" (feel out of control) when you start changing and growing. To restore their feelings of internal control and predictability others may subconsciously want to keep you the way you were, even if you were unhappy or unhealthy.

It is important to remember that all *modifiers* may temporarily create uncomfortable feelings. This is because solving a problem is *change*, and change generally involves moving outside one's *comfort zone* as mentioned previously.

It helps to remember that progressive movement in one's life will always have a short-lived period of adjustment that may be uncomfortable. It also helps to remember that this temporary discomfort is not near as uncomfortable as staying permanently in the old out-lived or destructive patterns.

Step 3-B
Shaping the modifier into a *Primary Domino Thought* (*PDT*)

The tool of transformation is the the *Primary Domino Thought*. Developing it is is similar to sharpening a tool for maximum efficiency.

This is a very critical part of the process. The *Primary Domino Thought* is truly the front line transformer. It is *the* workhorse, *the* change agent in action, *the* catalyst, and *the* thing that makes you a magician in creating your own life the way you want it. The actual *Primary Domino Thought* will manifest the shift in your problem without you having to manage all the little changes between the *modifier* and the desired outcome.

"*Shaping the modifier*" means shortening the *modifier* into images, numbers, or into a memorable linguistic form such as an easily remembered phrase. Cognitive science teaches us that the human mind easily stores/recalls only short pieces of information. Telephone numbers are 7 numbers in length because it is the maximum number of digits the human mind can easily remember.

The *modifier* must be shortened and sweetened to be effective into the *Primary Domino Thought* and should be "catchy" to the user. "Catchy" means that it has some sort of very subjective appeal to the user. The appeal is something that sort of clicks in when one finds it. Although it might not mean a thing to anyone else, for the user it encompasses the *modifier* and more. It has an emotional tug to it, an encompassing wholeness about it, perhaps even a gut level impact that this is *the* one. It is important to note that the Primary Domino Thought, or *PDT*, can be in many different forms:

a) **linguistic** = a word, phrase, or acronym

"sleek physique" if one is attempting to lose weight

"make merry" if one wants to uplift one's mood

"unlock block" to unleash creativity

"finesse stress" for making peace with tension

"soothingyouthing" to reduce aging

b) **numerical** = single number, number phrase, or formula

c) **symbols** = △, ♇;*; ☺ ;❀ ; ✝ ;♥ ; ◕; etc., etc.

d) **photographic snapshot**

e) **animated film clip**

f) **abstraction** = swirling colors, sliding geometric figures, etc.

g) **combination** = any of the above.

The only criteria for a good *Primary Domino Thought* is that it mentally represents the *modifier* so you have subjective feelings of identification with it.

Creativity in brevity is also encouraged in order to maximize impact. One reason why those sentence-length mental affirmations that were at one time popular were not very effective was because the "string" of words was too long for the subconscious mind to digest.

The best way to learn how to create *Primary Domino Thoughts* is to continue to play with them. Let yourself be creative and have some fun. When you have created an effective *Primary Domino Thought* you can easily tell by the "aha!" reaction you will feel inside. The *PDTs* you need will easily click in automatically once you get the hang of it.

There is virtually no limit on the number of potential *Primary Domino Thoughts* or to the areas you may wish to influence with them. They can be utilized for the narrowest of purposes, such as a headache or a thought pattern that you wish to change. *Primary Domino Thinking* is just as effective with more far-reaching and holistic lifestyle concerns, such as one's spiritual or financial development.

Step 3-C

Attach a timer, if relevant

Some *Primary Domino Thoughts* need a time frame. Example: If you desired to lose weight, you would want the subconscious mind to terminate the command at a predetermined ideal weight (e.g., 125 pounds), otherwise you would keep losing weight beyond the point of desirability. The fully stated *Primary Domino Thought* with *timer* might then be "SLEEK PHYSIQUE-125 LBS."

Example: If while in a 10K race you need extra energy, the command might be issued toward the end of the race. The fully stated *Primary Domino Thought* with *timer* inserted at the beginning of the last kilometer might be "***Emergency Energy -'Til The Tape.***"

Step 3 - Example:

After researching the topic of depression, Adam verifies to himself that he is, indeed, depressed. He has put on weight, he is angry most of the time, has occasional fantasies about the relief he would experience from dying, he has difficulties sleeping well, is getting compulsive, and he "doesn't play well with others." Basically, Adam feels helpless and hopeless.

Adam adopts a strategy of overcoming his helplessness and hopelessness by formulating the *modifier* "I easily, quickly and joyfully manifest what I need to be happy and healthy." After some trial and error to determine which feels right, Adam then converts the *modifier* into the *Primary Domino Thought* of a **snapshot** of himself trim, muscular, and with a bright confident smile on his face.

YOUR STORY:

A) Write your Step 2 problem explanation from page 97.

_____

_____

B) Convert your Step 2 problem explanation from page 97 into a *modifier*.

_____

_____

_____

C) Test the *modifier* against the Guidelines for Great Modifiers on page 105.

D) Shape the *modifier* into a *Primary Domino Thought* - a phrase, number, symbol, snapshot, animation, abstraction, or combination (see page 110).

_____

_____

E) Attach a *timer* if necessary (see page 111).

_____

CHAPTER 10

PRIMARY DOMINO THINKING
STEP 4

THE FIVE STEPS OF *PRIMARY DOMINO THINKING*

STEP 1: Passionate Possession

STEP 2: Exploration of the Problem or Issue

STEP 3: Producing the Primary Domino Thought

STEP 4: Primary Domino Thought Implantation

STEP 5: Regulation

PRIMARY DOMINO THOUGHT IMPLANTATION

Apply your secret formula.

All previous chapters and their explanations and preparations were important, because they bring us to this moment of truth about redesigning our lives: *Implementation*. This is where the rubber meets the road - the critical point of contact that will make all the deliberate differences you desire to make. Developing competence with

Step 4 will put you in the commander's seat of converting problems into solutions in your life.

Because Step 4 is the most critical of the steps, as well as the most challenging, it is important to carefully define the essential vocabulary. Please take your time and internalize the following terms and their meanings before moving to actual implementation. You don't have to memorize them, just understand them. This will maximize your benefits and minimize the number of trials it takes to achieve your goals.

Step 4 Glossary

Visualization = an internal picturing that is meaningful to you

There is no right or wrong way to visualize. *Primary Domino Thinking* depends on your natural ability to deliberately and symbolically represent situations internally. Some of your *PDT* colleagues have utilized pictures (snapshots), words or their acronyms (like a typewriter/word processor in action), cartoons/caricatures, symbols, abstractions of color and movement, or film clips (animation).

Whatever form of visualization is utilized, it is *the* means of conveying a message to your subconscious system, which then actually carries out the transformation desired by automatically setting up the rest of the "dominoes" (thoughts, behaviors and events) needed to create the outcome you desire.

Do you see the difference here? The reason most people are unsuccessful at manifesting the reality they want is because they have everything bassackwards. When they encounter an issue or problem they make up their minds in a split second as to a solution, grab onto a strategy they have used before (that probably didn't work very well then either!), and frustratingly attempting to arm wrestle a solution all the way through to the end result they think *should* be the outcome.

Instead, our dedication is in designing and setting up the correct *Primary Domino Thought* and then just sitting back and watching desired outcomes happen automatically. Got it?

****

Timeline = you experiencing life

There are two 'types' of time. *Linear time* is your past-present-future life in an apparent line. *Momentary time* is your consciousness (life) operating in the present moment, which is the only time in which it *can* operate.

From the latter perspective there really is no such thing as the past or future, there are only successive moments of NOW, i.e., *momentary time*. Of course, there *were* moments of NOW called the *past* and there *will be* moments of NOW called the *future*.

> *Your power rests solely in this moment and is represented by your conscious choice-making.*

You cannot make choices in the past or in the future. You can only make choices inthe moment. Yes, you can make choices about how you will regardthe past or the future, and these can be powerful choices indeed, but even then, those choices can *only* be made in the present moment. In other words, I can say, "You know, I guess it wasn't so bad getting fired that time when I was 25. It made me really look at where my life was heading." But I make that choice to regard that unpleasant past situation in a more pleasant light in the NOW.

It is the same with forecasting: I say to myself, "I can choose to see the future as scary or as exciting, so I think I'll see it as exciting." But I make that choice about the future in the NOW.

CLUE:

The more you are able to live in the present moment, the more power you have.

Question: When are you the least powerful?
Answer: When you are unconscious.
Consciousness works on a sliding scale: The further you are, in any moment, from being fully conscious, the less powerful you are. Step 4 is a fully-conscious-in-the-moment process.

> If you are having difficulty getting into the moment, conscious connected breathing will help you get HERE AND NOW very quickly. Just two or three connected breaths will pull you into present time. But don't stop there; it is best to do CCB throughout Step 4.

We use images in our heads to represent "reality" all the time. You need to choose an image, or *visualization*, that will represent your *timeline*, meaning *your life as it moves through its moments*. It should be something you can relate to wholistically, meaning something that "grabs" you. Here are some visualizations that people have used:

a) a transparent hollow tube (the structure of your life, past present and future) with water running through it (your life energy) and an opening through the top (representing where you are NOW);

b) a set of railroad tracks (the structure of your life, past present and future), and a moving flatcar (your life energy) with you standing in the middle of it (representing where you are NOW);

c) standing on the beach facing the sun on the ocean's horizon (the ocean represents the structure of your life, past present and future), the waves (your life energy) move away from the shore, and you cast a bottle (representing where you are NOW) with your *PDT* inside. As it reaches the sun it dissolves, becoming one with your life.

d) etc., you can create many visual metaphors representing the active present moment in your life. Take some time - maybe a day - and come up with one you can really relate to.

****

Thought = awareness in the here and now; thoughts are also tools for shaping (or refraining from shaping) experience

A *thought* is in the present moment. When you boil it down there is no awareness outside of *thoughts*. Within *thought* resides your consciousness, your experience, and all of your power. Your deliberate power is represented by conscious choice-making: *Primary Domino Thoughts*.

The way your life works (or doesn't) rests upon individual *thoughts*. This is wonderful, because a *thought* is the one thing you can totally control.* It is this realization, plus the design of the *thought* and the manner in which you implement it, that makes all the difference in your life. [* Premium mental health is synonymous with the ability to think clearly. The more "mentally ill" a person is, the less control they have of their thinking. Being out of control of our thinking is very painful because of the intense amount of fear involved. Many think a mentally ill person is in such pain that they cannot think straight when, in actuality, the reverse is true: The mentally ill are in pain because they cannot think straight. Bizarre behavior, which often accompanies mental illness, is a twisted attempt to deal with the psychic pain, which closely resembles a migraine of the soul. *Primary Domino Thinking can be very useful in helping to cure the mentally ill.*]

Internal representation of a *Primary Domino Thought*: Visualize it in the form of a phrase, a set of initials (acronym) of a phrase, a picture, an animation, or a symbol.

****

Implant = a Primary Domino Thought inserted into the timeline

An *implant* is the deliberate insertion of a well-defined *Primary Domino Thought* into the present moment. This is THE central tool of transformation. *Primary Domino Thought* is the noun; *implant* is the verb. You *implant* the *Primary Domino Thought* into your consciousness which is represented by your *timeline*.

****

Rimplant = a replacement implant which involves an extraction of an ongoing thought

When you are aware that an *implant* is replacing a negative or inappropriate thought, an extraction must be performed at the same time as *implantation*. This is very similar to replacing a defective organ or joint in the body; the bad part goes out and the new part goes in, only this time it is mental rather than physical. When a *Primary Domino Thought* is *implanted* at the same time an *extraction* occurs, it is known as a *rimplant*.

Internal representation of an active implant or rimplant: Any or all of the following utensils have proven useful as visualized methods of insertion into the visualized representation of your *timeline* (life experience): chisel; trowel; syringe (as in getting a healthy injection); pry bar; shovel; capsule; \ ; sliding board; etc.

****

Extraction = removal of a previously instituted implant

An *extraction* is the removal of a debilitating thought that is no longer desired, by visualizing its representation (picture, phrase, symbol, etc.) as being withdrawn. *Extraction* is the term utilized when one is only removing an old thought without inserting a new *Primary Domino Thought*. This is done primarily when one discovers old detrimental "head recordings" that have been driving one into destructive modes of behavior. Sometimes these are negative childhood *implants* placed in us by careless or ignorant authority figures, malevolent abusers, or institutions such as schools, religions, hospitals, etc.

Internal representation of an active extraction: Visualized tools for *extraction* can be the same ones utilized in *implantation*, only in reverse. Others that have been used are *visualizations* of pipettes; grappling hooks; steam shovels; siphons; forceps; / ; bulldozers; etc.

****

Emotion-sensation = concentration of energy around an emotion with the accompanying physical sensation

Any single human experience has three "doors" into it. Each experience you have is obviously recorded mentally, no matter how trivial or even unnoticed it may be, but each experience also has **emotional** evaluation and physical **sensation** components. We have a tendency to separate them out, but in actuality they are merely *perspectives* of the same experience.

Consider that you have never seen a fish or an aquarium. You walk into a room where there are three video monitors next to each other. Unknown to you, these monitors are connected to three video cameras in another room focused on the same aquarium which contains a single swimming fish. The first camera is focused on the side of the aquarium, the second on the end, and the third is above the aquarium looking straight down on top of the fish. As you gaze at the monitors you believe that three different fish are being monitored. Soon it dawns on you that they are moving in incredible harmony with each other. You deduce that these fish must have some means of very accurate communication as well as rigorous self-discipline. It is so unbelievable that you focus more and more on the similarities until, in a flash of insight, you realize that they are one in the same fish viewed from three different angles.

So it is with experience. We separate our experience into three pieces - *physical, mental, emotional* - for reasons of convenience or from habit, but all pieces are present regardless of our cognizance of them.

All one must do is reflect on this to know its truth. Some experiences such as eating seems very physical, but a little reflection easily brings the emotions and thoughts about the food to us. Watching your favorite sports team score is a very emotional experience - but, again, with a little reflection one can easily bring the thoughts and physical sensations to awareness. Perhaps a casual conversation isn't usually very dramatic, but again with careful reflection you could become aware of your mental, physical, and emotional experiencing during that conversation. Success with *Primary Domino Thinking* asks you to become more aware of all three doors into your experiencing of life.

Each person's physical response to each emotion is unique. When you are angry, you may feel a tightening in your chest or have a queasy stomach. When you feel joy, you may feel light in weight and your chest is relaxed. It is important for you to get to know just how you individually register your emotions in your body, so you can deliberately duplicate them later.

****

[End of Glossary]

MOST IMPORTANT!

Primary Domino Thoughts are only to be implanted
when one is in a moment of feeling 'good.'

This cannot be overemphasized.

Most humans, if they think at all to self-intervene, only do so when they are feeling badly. This is equivalent to casting seeds onto a flat rock and expecting them to grow. Your chances of success rise immeasurably if you plant the seeds in rich soil where they can take root, correct? The *Primary Domino Thought* is exactly like a seed, and it needs to be implanted at a moment when one feels uplifted and the mental soil is rich.

The challenge here is that most humans don't even think to deliberately influence their own lives when they are feeling good. This is often the major differentiation between beginners and those experienced with *Primary Domino Thinking*. Rookies see the 'good moment' as an opportunity to indulge as long as the ride lasts (which they feel won't be long); but when they get more experience the 'feeling good moment' is seen as not only a chance to gain control over the duration of the moment, but also an opening in which to *implant* and/or reinforce a number of *Primary Domino Thought*s to insure a bountiful future crop of positive healthy outcomes. The feeling good moment provides flat out opportunism with the highest of intentions and the ultimate of harvests.

CLUE:

If you wish to modify the metal, you must learn to strike while the iron is hot.

ANOTHER CLUE:

A successful person gets up in the morning looking for an opportunity and if there isn't one, makes it.

If you wish to get maximum benefit from *Primary Domino Thinking*, then also make an *implantation* regarding *willingness* to not only notice these fertile moments but also to take advantage of them when they are present.

How to Create the 'Good Moment'

You do not have to wait for a 'good moment.' You can create it. The idea of creating a 'good moment' is closely aligned with the ultimate goal of *Primary Domino Thinking*. In other words, if you are feeling poorly, and in that moment have a desire to do some deliberate self-design, the fertile ground can be created in several ways. Here are some popular and effective means by which one can create deliberate happiness.

Conscious Connected Breathing (CCB)

You can create the good moment by performing conscious connected breathing and relaxation until you feel uplifted, and *then* the *Primary Domino Thought* can be implanted!

CCB creates a "window" or space in which you take control of the situation (this helps right away), inhale large amounts of fresh air (this helps), eliminate a lot of waste product through the exhale (this helps), send a message to the autonomic nervous system that everything is OK (this really helps!), and induce elimination of the source of most pain, which is ultimately your resistance (this helps a whole way big bunch!), and then the relaxation signifies a readiness to make a shift. And this is all within your control no matter what is going on in the outside world! It just takes *willingness* to do it.

Shifting contexts

Another method of creating 'good moments' is by deliberately shifting contexts. We know how to do this, but we rarely do it regularly and deliberately. A *context* is the way in which we regard something. I can choose to see a flat tire many ways: a painful experience; a race to see how fast I can change the tire; a challenge to find and use the owner's manual; a chance to use my AAA dues; an opportunity to meet a passing motorist; a good story for later on; etc. It is totally up to me how I wish to experience this flat tire. Oh, and I can also choose to react the same way I always do by staying angry at the inconvenience (after all, this tactic works so well!).

The point is, if I'm feeling badly, it has a lot to do with how I am choosing to view the situation that I am in, and I can change how I feel by changing how I regard the situation.

Want to prove you can do it? Sit and do CCB for 30 seconds and then reflect on a situation in your life for which you could alter your view, then do so in as many ways as you can. Be creative, weird, or outlandish just have fun with this. Humor is highly recommended. Notice how your body and emotions change with each new context. Practice doing this with daily situations for the next week and notice the dramatic results. One client, constantly annoyed by a power-tripping obnoxious boss, began to visualize him naked every time she saw him. Think about it.

Humor

Another method of inducing a "feeling good" moment is through direct application of humor. Remember, you don't have to feel good to laugh...you can laugh in order to feel good. Some clients keep humorous books around (Calvin & Hobbes books are some of my favorites) to pull out and read on specific occasions when a shift is needed. You can also visualize other things that make you smile, such as cute clumsy puppies, a Charlie Chaplin sequence, or any humorous memory.

Pleasant Memories

When you are not having a good moment but you want to create one, do this: Sit with your eyes closed and vividly remember a pleasant moment in your life. Picture the scenery, yourself in it, and remember all the details including the emotions that went with it. Do some CCB along with this for two minutes and notice what happens! Try it right now.

Once the good moment is present, or created, move on to Step 4 of *Primary Domino Thinking.*

****

Step 4-A

Visualize implantation (and extraction, if relevant) of the *Primary Domino Thought* with *timer*

While relaxing the body and performing conscious connected breathing, *implant* the *Primary Domino Thought* along with the *timer* into the *timeline*, represented by whatever you have chosen to represent your experiencing of life in the NOW. Do this by first visualizing the *Primary Domino Thought*. If one is replacing a former thought, or*implant*, then the old thinking must be visualized as being extracted before the new thinking is implanted. Again, possible ways in which a *Primary Domino Thought* can be represented internally include:

a) Visualizing the actual words, or their acronym

b) Visualizing an actual photograph or snapshot

c) Visualizing a cartoon-like or caricature-like pictorial

d) Visualizing an abstraction such as moving colors

e) Visualizing numerical characters

f) Visualizing a film clip, or animation

g) Visualizing a symbol

h) Utilizing a combination of any or all of the above.

It is extremely important to *visualize* the *Primary Domino Thought* being inserted with a tool such as a chisel, shovel, trowel, syringe, etc. or entering your body with each inhale. In the beginning one should probably do this with the eyes closed and in a relaxed state (obviously not while driving or operating your favorite bulldozer).

Maximum efficiency with *Primary Domino Thinking* is obtained by doing Step 4a minimum of 5 minutes a day, remembering to accompany the *implant* with conscious connected breathing and relaxation.

Step 4-B
Generating the emotion of accomplishment

Along with the breathing and relaxing, effectiveness is dramatically increased by *activating* (bringing up from within) the emotional counterparts that would accompany the actual realization of the solution to your problem(*modifier*). Just in case the previous sentence was confusing: The more total your involvement in bringing the new results into fruition, the more effective the outcome.

Generating emotion is a very powerful entry into the subconscious mind. It involves avenues of communication monitored by the subconscious/autonomic nervous system. This bypasses the conscious system which has often been responsible for keeping you locked into the thoughts which have created the need for this re-engineering session in the first place!

Some examples of generated emotion would be: a) the emotion of elation upon feeling a sudden burst of energy; b) the joyous self-confidence of being twenty-five pounds lighter; or, c) the serenity of an alleviated headache.

These actualizations of emotion-sensation should be done in tandem with the visualized *implantation* of the *Primary Domino Thought*. In other words, Step 4 - A, B, C, should all be done at the same time.

Step 4-C

Generating the physical sensations of accomplishment

Imagine the physical sensations that would go with successful accomplishment as if the *Primary Domino Thought* had already come true. Place yourself inside the *visualization.* Posture your body accordingly. If vitality is your goal, then at the time of *implantation* let your body get erect, head up, eyes bright and eager while breathing fully in an energized fashion. If becoming slimmer is the *modifier*, then imagine how your body would feel at that ideal weight. Can you feel the lightness, the relaxation in your tissues from not having to carry all that weight, the electricity in your body from being successful at something you thought would never happen? See yourself as slimmer and feel the emotions that go with it. Get into it!

IMPORTANT: Practice

The three parts of Step 4 should be performed daily for a minimum of 5 continuous minutes, reshaping them as you learn of more effective forms, until they are absorbed naturally into your experience. There they can be savored and enjoyed. It cannot be overemphasized how valuable patience, persistence and a sense of adventure can be in the successful implementation of Step 4.

Slack periods will now disappear for you. During the day while waiting in line, in an office for an appointment, at a railroad crossing, under the hair dryer, during commercials, at the car wash, on the subway, at the airport, on telephone-hold, etc., take advantage and fill these moments with CCB and implantation of your *Primary Domino Thought*. These now become great moments of productivity rather than a "waste of time."

Remember, when you feel "good" to take advantage and implant one or more *Primary Domino Thoughts* - these are tillable moments when the soil is just right for harvesting a rich crop later on!

IMPORTANT: Journaling

I must say that my clients have had much better results when after they do their 5 minute a day session that they keep a notebook nearby and journal just a paragraph or two about their experience. What to write? Oh, how the session went - what worked, what didn't, ideas, insights, etc. This seems to be a very powerful self-teaching tool, and keeps you not only from making the same errors twice, but also speeds up the achievement of your goals.

Journaling is so beneficial that I am tempted to say the process of *Primary Domino Thinking* requires you to do this, except I know of people who have had success without it. I say try it both ways if you are serious enough to really perfect this process and tailor it to your particular style.

Step 4 - Example

Adam adopted a strategy of overcoming his helplessness and hopelessness by formulating the *modifier* "I easily, quickly and joyfully manifest what I need to be happy and healthy." And converted it into the *Primary Domino Thought* of a **snapshot** of himself trim, muscular, and with a bright confident smile on his face.

Every morning Adam rises ten minutes earlier than usual and sits erect doing conscious connected breathing. When he feel awake, alert, refreshed and positive he visualizes the *Primary Domino Thought* snapshot of himself placed in a bottle and implants it by tossing it into the ocean and watches it gently wash out to sea and melt into the sun. He lets himself emotionally and physically feel *as if* he is already trim, muscular, and wearing a bright confident smile representing his new non-depressed way of life. After enjoying this implantation for 5 minutes he takes out his journal and logs down his experiences.

YOUR STORY:

A) Create a visualization of your *Primary Domino Thought*.

_____

_____

B) Create the good moment through CCB, shifting contexts, humor, or a pleasant memory.

C) *Implant* the *Primary Domino Thought*.

D) Feel the emotions of accomplishment.

E) Feel the physical sensations of accomplishment.

F) Journal your results, including actual experiences, problems if any, possible remedies and feelings.

CHAPTER 11

PRIMARY DOMINO THINKING
STEP 5

THE FIVE STEPS OF PRIMARY DOMINO THINKING

STEP 1: Passionate Possession

STEP 2: Exploration of the Problem or Issue

STEP 3: Producing the Primary Domino Thought

STEP 4: Primary Domino Thought Implantation

STEP 5: Regulation

REGULATION

"Monitoring and adjusting makes the difference."

The 5th Step is not always necessary, *but* if it is needed it is imperative. The more experience you have with *Primary Domino Thinking* the less you will need this step because you will have your life

---

right where you want it most of the time. This may or may not be long in coming.

For now, know that if you don't get the results you want, then the 5th Step is critical to refining your application of the process until you are totally satisfied. Continue to repeat and refine Steps 1 - 4 until you acquire precision and effectiveness with *Primary Domino Thinking*.

Step 5 completes the essential loop of feedback and refinement between goals and outcomes. It provides a space to reflect upon what you hoped would happen and what actually did happen. It provides an opportunity to continue and/or modify the pursuit of your purpose. As previously mentioned, you are strongly encouraged to "journal your journey" with *Primary Domino Thinking* - especially with the next process.

How to Do Step 5 - The Checklist

A. What was the change desired?

B. What *modifier* was selected to bring about the change?

C. What *Primary Domino Thought* was utilized?

D. Was a *timer* indicated?

E. Was *implantation* carried out with *visualization*?

F. Was *implantation* carried out with the emotion of accomplishment?

G. Was *implantation* carried out with the physical sensations of accomplishment?

H. What unforeseen benefits occurred outside my purpose?

I. What unforeseen challenge occurred outside my purpose?

J. Were there additional areas or objectives uncovered during the process?

K. Were my results satisfactory?

L. If not, should A - E be modified and in what manner?

M. Do the 5-steps again.

It is indeed possible for a single application of a *Primary Domino Thought* to create the long-term results you desire. Excellent results in just one application frequently happen, and there is absolutely no good reason why they shouldn't happen every time. There are plenty of not-so-good reasons, however, and in these cases it will take a persistent and patient effort at repeating and refining the *modifier* and the derived *Primary Domino Thought* until success is achieved. You *will* learn from these adjustments. You will learn how to be efficient and effective in applying *Primary Domino Thinking*.

By working through Steps 1 - 4 you will always arrive at the correct destination. Your accuracy in appraisal and application increases with persistent *awareness* and *willingness*. Be willing to take action again and again, if necessary. **Never give up.**

A Note About Results

That *Primary Domino Thinking* works is irrefutable because there are so many success stories, but exactly *how* the results exhibit themselves is variable, not only from person to person, but from application to application within a person. It is good advice to let go of the need to arm wrestle the results from the process (as 'science' erroneously attempts to do) and concentrate on the process itself.

> Ride easy in the saddle with controlling results; just persistently do your best and leave the rest.

Results with *Primary Domino Thinking* run the continuum from *instant* all the way to *gradual*. Mood changes can occur in an eye-blink. Have you ever experienced "insight," or suddenly had a "change of heart"? Have you ever been in one mood, heard a song on the radio, and then been suddenly transported into another mood? You now can make these shifts deliberately by internalizing the five steps of *Primary Domino Thinking*, and using it whenever you prefer another mood. Body sensations can be altered the same way. You have experienced, no doubt, the sudden onset or cessation of an itch, twitch, tension, or any muscular movement. The sensation is suddenly there and then, just as suddenly, it is not. You can now deliberately create and delete physical sensations. Thoughts are suddenly there, and then they are not. You can choose this outcome as well. A little practice and persistence and you can master all of these functions at will. By mastering mood, sensation and thought, you master the world.

Some areas of behavioral change will perhaps take longer because you have identified the wrong cause and, therefore, need to heed Step 5 rigorously. *Lack of results is a major clue.* The process cannot be "wrong" for you - it can only be applied correctly and effectively or incorrectly and less effectively. Some areas of behavior will take longer because they are complex, and you will discover all the "subparts" that need addressing as you go.

Don't be disheartened when things don't snap right into place as you expected - see it as an adventure. You *are* safe and you *are* doubtlessly going to wind up in a better place, even if you cannot always predict exactly where. So, you may think the problem of thirty pounds you have put on is why your spouse has lost interest in your sex life, and you perform *Primary Domino Thinking* to lose the 30 pounds, only to find out that it wasn't the weight, but something else that needs addressing. Thus, what has happened here?

- You lost 30 pounds;
- You found out you *can dothat* on your own;
- You have more confidence in yourself (overcoming 30 pounds is a very tangible confidence builder!);
- You are more adept at *Primary Domino Thinking* (overcoming 30 pounds is a very tangible skills builder!); and, very importantly,
- You may now correctly identify *the* problem and have a proven vehicle with which to do something about it!

The journey *is* successful. Although the exact outcome was never predicted by you in the beginning, without the beginning there could not have been a successful outcome!

Sometimes results are highly visible only in retrospect. Often at the Institute for Transformational Studies we receive calls, letters, e-mail, comments from amazed people saying, "I just noticed that : a) I don't have the urge to smoke/drink/etc. anymore; b) I don't have those crazy feelings anymore; c) I don't have those obsessive thoughts anymore about insecurity/work/my children/money /etc.; or, d) My lower backaches have been gone for three days/my body is healing so rapidly [in various ways]/my headaches are gone/etc." These delayed results are a thrill, much like unexpectedly receiving a holiday gift in the mail a week late. They are also a tribute to the true power of a single thought when thoughtfully applied.

EXAMPLE:

Adam knows that he has found the right *Primary Domino Thought* because he notices opportunities constantly manifesting with no dedicated work other than the 10 minutes every morning. Certain helpful books, people, and ideas practically materialize in front of him. As he merely takes advantage of these offerings and intuitively follows the new thoughts that are materializing, Adam sees himself becoming more and more like his *PDT*: trim, muscular, and with a genuine bright confident smile on his face.

Despite his primary success with *Primary Domino Thinking*, Adam will forget to use it many other times when it could benefit him. It is with time and practice that he will a) notice the situations where *Primary Domino Thinking* could work for him; and, b) apply *PDT* more and more efficiently, effectively and quickly.

YOUR STORY:

What will be the rest of the your story? Is it not now totally up to you? You may not know the answers but you *do* know the means to find them. How will the middle dominos show up without your trying to "figure it all out"? No one knows, but after you have several successful experiences with *Primary Domino Thinking* your faith and confidence will be dramatically increased and will carry you confidently onwards.

How will you remember to use this new powerful tool? Sometimes it will be memory that reminds you of *Primary Domino Thinking's* useful existence. Sometimes it will be emotional pain that causes you to remember the relief available.

Often a sense of energizing empowerment will arrive through consciousness of a single breath. The awareness of that single breath creates the window of opportunity, the moment rich with power for you to create your happiness.

CHAPTER 12

CONCLUSION

THE FIVE STEPS OF *PRIMARY DOMINO THINKING*

STEP 1: Passionate Possession

To have impact, you must dare to get close.

___Have you passionately possessed the problem by being willing to accept it as your experience alone?

___Are you mentally ready to take full responsibility for solving this problem?

___Are you doing Conscious Connected Breathing so that your body is exhibiting acceptance of the problem?

STEP 2:Exploration of the Problem or Issue

Investigate the problem, discovering who truly owns it.

___Have you thoroughly considered the possible causes of your problem?

___From all the possible causes have you selected the one that feels most correct?

___Have you stated the most accurate explanation for your problem?

___Are you positive that the problem is yours and yours alone?

___Is the problem clearly and succinctly stated?

STEP 3:Producing the Primary Domino Thought

Generate your secret formula.

___Have you converted your problem statement into its positive mirror image, or *modifier*?

___Does your modifier meet these guidelines?

    a) It is significant to me.

    b) It is clear to me.

    c) It seems complete to me.

    d) It is specific.

    e) It is precise.

    f) It is stated in the present tense.

    g) It is personally stated (the pronoun "I" is used, if any).

___Have you shaped the *modifier* statement into a *Primary Domino Thought* representative symbol, phrase, graphic, etc.?

___If necessary, have you attached a *timer*?

STEP 4: Primary Domino Thought Implantation

Apply your secret formula.

___Have you created the good moment by doing CCB, shifting contexts, using humor, or remembering something pleasant?

___Did you visualize the implantation/rimplantation of your *Primary Domino Thought* and *timer*?

___Did you generate the emotion of accomplishment?

___Did you generate the physical sensations of accomplishment?

STEP 5:Regulation

Monitoring and adjusting makes the difference.

___Use the Step 5 Checklist to refine your procedure.

___A. What was the change desired?

___B. What *modifier* was selected to bring about the change?

___C. What *Primary Domino Thought* was utilized?

___D. Was a *timer* indicated?

___E. Was *implantation* carried out with *visualization*?

___F. Was *implantation* carried out with the emotion of accomplishment?

___G. Was *implantation* carried out with the physical sensations of accomplishment?

___H. What unforeseen benefits occurred outside my

purpose?

___I. What unforeseen challenges occurred outside my purpose?

___J. Were there additional areas or objectives uncovered

during the process?

___K. Were results satisfactory?

___L. If not, in what manner should A - E be modified?

___M. Do the 5-steps again.

Designing Your World

Primary Domino Thinking, and the empowerment it represents, is indicative of a significant paradigm shift for our times. If *Primary Domino Thinking* becomes powerful enough (time will tell us about this) it may eventually be seen as a significant means to help end human suffering as we know it. If this is to be true it will start with people just like you, deciding to design and implement elegant thinking on a deliberate basis. It will be because of people just like you, consciously and conscientiously applying *Primary Domino Thoughts* to create health, wealth, and happiness. It will be because of people just like you, proving on a daily basis that:

MISERY IS OPTIONAL!

BIBLIOGRAPHY

Allen, James. *As A Man Thinket*h. Stamford, CT. Longmeadow
    Press, 1993.

Armstrong, Thomas. *7 Kinds of Smart*. New York: Penguin.
1993.

Bennett, Hal Zina& Sparrow, Susan. *Follow Your Bliss.* New
    York: Avon Books, 1990.

Benz, Dyrian& Weiss, Halko. *To The Core of Your Experience.*
    Charlottesville, VA: Luminas Press, 1989.

Biffle, Christopher. *The Castle of The Pearl.* New York: Harper
    & Row, 1990.

Bradshaw, John. *Healing The Shame That Binds You.* Videotape
    Presentation, PBS. 1991.

Campbell, Peter A. &McMahhon, Edwin M. *Bio-Spirituality:
    Focusing As A Way To Grow.* Chicago: Loyola
    University Press, 1985.

Capra, Fritjof. *The Tao of Physics.* Boston: Shambhala,1991.

Carlsen, Mary B. *Meaning-Making: Therapeutic Processes in
    Adult Development.* New York: w.w. Norton &
    Co.,1988.

Chopra, Deepak. *Unconditional Life: Discovering the Power to
    Fulfill Your Dreams.* New York: Bantam, 1992.

_____. [Anything written by Deepak is golden.]

Cousins, Norman. *Head First...The Biology of Hop*e. New York:
    E. P. Dutton, 1989.

Dallmann-Jones, A. S. &The Black River Group. *The Expert Educator...A Reference Manual of Teaching Strategies for Quality Education.* Fond du Lac, WI: Three Blue Herons Publishing, Inc., 1994.

Dallmann-Jones, A. S. &Osterhaus, R. *Is Education Having A Heart Attack...Eight Symptoms and A Plan for Rehabilitation.* Fond du Lac, WI: Three Blue Herons Pub., Inc., 1994.

Dallmann-Jones, A. S. *Living A Stress Free Life.* Fond du Lac, WI: Wolf Creek Press. 1999.

Dossey, Larry, M.D. *Space, Time & Medicine.* Boston: New Science Library, 1982.

Eliade, Mircea. *Shamanism: Archaic Techniques of Ecstasy.*Princeton, N.J.: Princeton University Press. 1964

Ellis, Albert & Harper, Robert. *A Guide To Rational Living.* No. Hollywood, CA: Wilshire Book Co., 1973.

Ferguson, Marilyn. *The Aquarian Conspiracy: Personal and Social Transformation in Our Time.* New York: J. P. Tarcher. 1980.

FM-2030. *Are You A Transhuman?* New York: Warner Bros., 1989.

Gawain, Shakti. *Creative Visualization.* New York: Bantam Books, 1985.

_____. *The Path of Transformation.* Mill Valley, CA: Nataraj Pub. 1993.

Geber, Marcelle. "The Psycho-Motor Development of African Children in the First Year and the Influence of Maternal Behavior." *Journal of Social Psychology*, No. 47 (1958): 185-195.

Gershon, D. & Straub, Gail. *Empowerment.* New York: Dell, 1989.

Gleick, James. *Chaos: Making A New Science.* New York: Penguin, 1987.

Goswami, Amit. *The Self-Aware Universe.* New York: G. P. Putnam's Sons, 1993.

Grof, Stanislav&Binnet, Hal Z. *The Holotropic Mind.* New York: HarperCollins, 1992.

Hall, Edward T.*Beyond Culture.* New York: Doubleday, 1981.

Harvey, Bill. *Mind Magic.* New York: Unlimited Publishing, 1982. Hay, Louise. *The Power Is Within You.* Carson, CA: Hay House,

Inc.,1991.

Helmstetter, Shad. *Choices.* New York: Pocket Books, 1989.

Helmstetter, Shad. *What To Say When You Talk To Yourself.* New York: Pocket Books, 1982.

Herbert, Nick. *Elemental Min*d. New York: Penguin, 1993.

Howard, Vernon. *The Power of Your Supermind.* Marina del Ray, CA: DeVorss & Co., 1975.

Hua-Ching Ni. *Internal Alchemy.* Santa Monica, CA: The Shrine of the Eternal Breath of Tao, 1992.

Johanson, Greg & Kurtz, Ron. *Grace Unfolding: Psychotherapy in the Spirit of Tao-teChing.* New York: Bell Tower, 1991.

Kenyon, Tom. *Brain States.* Naples, FL: United States Publishing, 1994.

Langer, Ellen. *Mindfulness.* New York: Addison-Wesley Pub. Co., Inc. 1989.

Leonard, Jim. *Your Fondest Drea*m. Cincinnati: AVP Publishing, 1989.

Leonard, Jim &Laut, Phil.*Vivation: The Science of Enjoying All of Your Life*. Cincinnati: AVP Publishing, 1991.

Lilly, John & Lilly, Antonietta. *The Dyadic Cyclone*. New York: Simon & Schuster, 1976.

_____. [Anything written by John Lilly]

Lynch, Dudley &Kordis, Paul L. *Strategy of the Dolphin: Scoring A Win in A Chaotic World*. New York: Wm. Morrow & Co., 1988.

Maltz, Maxwell. *The Magic Power of Self-Image Psychology*. New York: Pocket Books, 1964.

Maslow, Abraham. *The Farther Reaches of Human Nature*. New York: Viking. 1971.

Millman, Dan. *The Way of The Peaceful Warrior*. Tiburon, CA: H.J. Kramer, Inc., 1984.

Moore, Thomas. *Care of The Soul*. New York: HarperCollins Publishers, 1992.

Peale, Norman Vincent. *You Can If You Think You Can*. Carmel, NY: Guideposts Assoc., Inc., 1974.

Pearce, Joseph C. *Magical Child*. Toronto: Clarke, Irwin & Co., 1977.

Penrose, Roger. *The Emperor's New Mind*. New York: Penguin Books. 1989.

Robbins, Tom. *Jitterbug Perfume*. New York: Bantam, 1985.

Robinson, Bryan. *Heal Your Self-Esteem: Recovery From Addictive Thinking*. Deerfield Beach, FL: Health Communications.

Small, Jacquelyn. *Transformers: The Therapists of the Future.* Marina Del Ray, CA: DeVorss& Co., 1982.

Smothermon, Ron. *Transforming # 1.* San Francisco: Context Publications, 1982.

Spencer-Brown, G. *Laws of Form.* New York: E. P. Dutton, 1979.

Talbot, Michael. *The Holographic Universe.* New York: Harper Collins, 1991.

Tae Yun Kim. *Seven Steps To Inner Power.* San Rafael, CA:New World Library, 1991.

Thompson, William I. *Imaginary Landscape: Making Worlds of Myth and Science.* New York: St. Martin's Press, 1989.

Paul, Richard. *Critical Thinking: What Every Person Needs To Survive In A Rapidly Changing World.* Santa Rosa, CA: Foundation for Critical Thinking, 1992.

Smith, Lester. *Inner Adventures.* Wheaton, IL: The Theosophical Publishing House, 1988.

Woolf, V. Vernon. *Holodynamics.* New York: Harbinger House, 1990.

Watts, Alan. *Cloud-Hidden, Whereabouts Unknown.* New York:Pantheon Books, 1973.

_____. [Anything else written by Alan, ever.]

Wegner, Daniel. *White Bears & Other Unwanted Thoughts.* New York: Viking, 1989.

Wilde, Stuart. *Affirmations.* Taos, NM: White Dove, 1987.

_____. [Anything else written by Stuart, ever.]

Zukav, Gary. The Seat of The Soul. New York: Simon & Schuster, 1990.

_____

_____

You are encouraged to participate in Dr. Dallmann-Jones' live *Primary Domino Thinking Seminars* offered in locations around the globe. Please write for a schedule of his appearances, or for information on sponsoring a workshop.

_____

_____

DZ Productions

Fond du Lac, Wisconsin 54937

www.SuccessHappinessPeace.com

Facebook.com/SHPCaptainsLog

Mission Statement: *DZ productions exists to research, develop and produce vehicles, bridges and scaffoldings that transform knowledge into productive intelligence for the betterment of humankind.*

Want a bit of feedback or need help on the PDT process?

Send your Problem Statement, your *modifier* and your Primary Domino Thought to Anthony@DrD-J.com for free feedback.

Especially if you are having trouble with the process!

www.ingramcontent.com/pod-product-compliance
Lightning Source LLC
Chambersburg PA
CBHW070806100426
42742CB00012B/2266